PARK RANGER

TRUE STORIES FROM A RANGER'S CAREER
IN AMERICA'S NATIONAL PARKS

Nancy Eileen Muleady-Mecham

VTP
Vishnu Temple Press • Flagstaff, AZ

ISBN 0-9674595-4-0
LCCN 2004103974

Cover and author photograph: Sean Brady
Cover design and book layout: Sandra Kim Muleady
All photos are from the author's personal collection
unless otherwise noted.

Vishnu Temple Press, LLC
P.O. Box 30821
Flagstaff, AZ 86003-0821
www.vishnutemplepress.com

Second Printing, January 2006

PRINTED IN THE UNITED STATES OF AMERICA

♣

For Mom, Eileen Shelley Muleady

CONTENTS

ACKNOWLEDGEMENTS

Many people have been supportive in my life as well as in the production of this book. Dr. Tom Myers was an inspiration and mentor. Tom Martin and Hazel Clark were guiding lights and the owners of Vishnu Temple Press. All of my family were instrumental in listening to and encouraging my stories. In particular, the following read early versions of the stories and provided positive feedback that led to this book: Kate and Bob Seager, Sheila and Steve Girardi, Danny and Gail Muleady, Jack Muleady and Kris Justus, Michelle Busby and Danielle Seager Frerichs, Bobby and Sandy Muleady, Kent Mecham, Mary Anne Carlton, and my Mom and Dad, Tom and Eileen Muleady. I also want to thank the following for their editorial expertise: Dr. Kris Justus, who also suggested the glossary, Sandra Kim Muleady, Mary Anne Carlton, and Hazel Clark. Sandra Kim Muleady performed the incredible graphic designs for the cover and typesetting. I would also like to thank the following for remembering details of some of the stories after they read them: Tim and Karen White, Nancy Hagerman, Jim Coffey, George Durkee and Paige Meier. A special thank you to Florie Takaki, John Mattox and Glenn Martin. I also want to thank Jack Davis, who was my Superintendent in Sequoia and Grand Canyon National Parks. Forever thanks to my parents, Eileen and Tom.

INTRODUCTION

W ith a biology degree fresh from UCLA, I had applied for
several jobs. In one interview, I was told my job would be
an environmental impact specialist. I was shown an office
in a basement without windows and told my duties included
reading reports and studies, then making recommendations. It
was a permanent job with the U.S. Government at mid-level
entry pay. At the end of the interview I was offered the job. I
drove to my parents' home to talk to my Mom. I could always
talk to her and she was always encouraging. When I arrived, she
told me I had a message from the U.S. Forest Service in the
Sierra National Forest. I returned the call and the hiring official
was blunt but clear. It was only a seasonal position at the lowest
pay for the job. I would work hard long hours of manual labor,
outside. I would be the only woman, in fact, the first in the
District. Did I want to be a wildland firefighter on an initial
attack engine crew? Absolutely!

I went to Dinkey Creek that summer and was trained as a
wildland firefighter in the classroom and in the field. It was 1977,
the year of some pretty big fires in California. I like to say I cut
enough fire line with my pulaski to go around the world. I

learned how to use and maintain tools, engines and hoselines. I also learned that, as a woman, I was not initially welcome. But I pulled my own weight and then some, and was in the best physical shape of my entire life. The next summer I returned, this time as a backcountry ranger, firefighter and sawyer. In 1979, I started seasonal work with the U.S. National Park Service.

I worked summers in Sequoia National Park and spent my winters either in a "winter park" (a park whose visitation peaks in the winter) or in school or as a city paramedic. Over the next two decades, I worked as a Ranger Naturalist as well as a Protection Ranger. Many parks had very few Protection Rangers, and Naturalist Rangers were (and still are) pressed into duty as Emergency Medical Technicians, Structural Fire Brigade members and other traditional protection duties. Eventually, I became a permanent ranger, specializing in protection, and over time, with schooling at training sessions and academies, advanced to the highest level in each of the duties a ranger is required to perform. It was daunting at times to realize that no matter what happened in my park, I might be the person who had to solve the problem or answer the call. I was a Federal Law Enforcement Officer, a Paramedic/Registered Nurse, Captain and Engineer on the Structural Fire Brigade, Medical Unit Leader for Wildland Fire, a Technical Search and Rescue Team member with specialties in helicopter shorthaul and swiftwater rescue, and a resource manager with B.A., M.A. and Ph.D. degrees in Biology.

A Protection Ranger is told he/she is there to protect the resources. But at bigger parks, there is barely time to note the resources because of the issues and baggage that millions of visitors bring with them. For example, on a resource horse patrol in Grand Canyon one day, I was riding through a parking lot to get to the rim of the canyon when I witnessed a woman swing a disposable camera through the air and whack her spouse on the side of his head. He was stunned long enough for her to race to the car and lock herself in with her two small children. The words out of his mouth would make a sailor blush. He would not stop yelling until he turned around and saw all of the horseflesh in front of him back him up against the car. That was a day involving assault, child protective services and counseling. I never got off of my horse and I didn't leave the parking lot for hours.

But when you do get into the resource, you realize what a spectacular concept National Parks are and how lucky you are to be a part of it. These are the resources that draw hundreds of millions of visitors a year. While I have always maintained that my primary job was the resource, I was the "service" in National Park Service. These stories are pulled from a variety of parks and circumstances, and show just how very involved that service can be.

Nancy Eileen Muleady-Mecham
Grand Canyon National Park, 2004

The Runner

I had always wanted to see a glacier. I had seen what they'd created in the granite block of the Sierra Nevada. Glaciers carved the U-shaped canyons, polished the slick rock, often with long scratches, and delivered boulders the size of houses to bizarre spots throughout the mountains. There had been numerous opportunities for glaciers to form in these western mountains in the past. All it took was more snow to accumulate into ice than had melted. Then the ice had to move. That was a glacier. Carving its way a millimeter at a time over eons, glaciers shaped the valleys and arêtes, and left moraines at its sides and end. Then, when it melted back, the deeply gouged hole at its origin filled with water instead of ice. These tarns were the thousands of lakes that dotted the high country of Sequoia and Kings Canyon National Parks.

I wasn't the only one that backpacked into this gorgeous high country of endless granite. Thousands of visitors from all walks of life put a backpack on and hit the hundreds of miles of trails in these two parks. Some of the more adventurous went further: the

John Muir Trail can take you north to Yosemite National Park and the Pacific Crest Trail runs from Canada to Mexico through the Parks.

I usually left for the backcountry on a weekend right after getting off work at Lodgepole in Sequoia National Park. I lived on a porch – a screened-in porch that faced east to the Watchtower that loomed over the cascading Marble Fork of the Kaweah River. I could step out my door and walk straight up the steep hill to the Twin Lakes Trail. The hill geologically is a moraine. It is composed of debris from a glacier that plowed through the Lodgepole area. One day, with the hope of joining friends for a night of star watching and camaraderie, I hit the High Sierra Trail at 6:00 p.m. with my pack and moved rapidly to Bearpaw Meadow 11.5 miles out. I arrived before 11:00 p.m. and could see the avalanche chutes of the Great Western Divide in the moonlight.

I absolutely understood the lure of the backcountry, preferring to share the hike with good friends. But if no one was available, I didn't hesitate to solo hike. There are added risks to hiking by yourself, and you always need to be diligent and make good choices. Should something happen, you cannot always rely on the kindness of strangers to help you. Not that there wasn't an unwritten code in the backcountry. Most will help another hiker in distress. But the distressed solo hiker has to find these strangers if he/she is to have any chance. The terrain of the High Sierra backcountry is so vast, the further you are from a trailhead, the fewer hikers you are likely to encounter.

It was just about lunchtime when backpackers Tim and Karen sat down to grab a bite to eat. They had hiked quite a bit already this trip. Through Le Conte Canyon from Evolution Valley, they had just finished climbing The Golden Staircase. The trail paralleled Palisade Creek as it climbed from 8,000 to 11,000 feet up to the Palisade Lakes. The trail was strenuous and strewn with granite boulders. There was nothing "golden" about the climb up; it was tough. But occasionally columbine flowers, with their yellow hue, nestled up against the sides of granite boulders and gave a hint of gold.

A solo hiker, Chuck, had caught up with Tim and Karen when a group of older hikers, coming down the trail, created a virtual traffic jam. It was an uncommon moment, but pleasantries were exchanged. The older hikers said they were retired and were having the time of their lives. There were three at this lunch spot, with two more stragglers to follow. Soon, the straggling two arrived. They were older ladies with a look of concern on their faces. They had fallen behind because they thought they had heard voices. Beyond the snickers of the moment of high altitude psychosis, they insisted they had thought they heard someone yelling, but could not pinpoint the origin. In the open basin of Palisade Lakes, there were enough opportunities for echoes and poor acoustics to make that possible. These older ladies convinced Chuck, Tim and Karen that something could be wrong, and the three set out, up the rest of the trail and across the basin. Chuck was able to out-distance the others and was scanning the slopes, passes and irregular hills that dotted the landscape. There were no trees, just an open and continuous expanse of granite in all directions. It was by no means flat either. The dusty trail of pulverized granite wound its way through huge slabs and small dips. After about twenty minutes, Chuck spotted something dark near the trail and in seconds realized it was a man, sprawled face down and lying in a pool of blood.

Dan was a 25-year-old Californian who loved to hike and to take photos. He didn't let the lack of a hiking partner stop him on this trip. When he entered the incredible Palisade Lakes area of the backcountry, it was spectacular. It was his fourteenth day of an extended trip and he wanted to photograph it all in one shot, to show the dwarfing immensity of it all. Dan left the trail and started off cross-country to a small mountain and up a northeast-facing avalanche chute. Another hiker stopped and called to Dan that he thought the chute looked dangerous. Dan reassured him that he was fine and the backpacker continued on. Dan soon took off his backpack and, with his camera and tripod, began to boulder hop and climb up the talus slope to frame his shot.

That's when the rock came loose. It plowed down onto his body and sent Dan into a free fall of ten feet, then a rolling, scattered fall farther down the jumble of sharp rocks. Dan didn't know how long he had been knocked unconscious. When he came to, he realized his left ankle was badly swollen and bruised. Then the pain and ache seared at him as he looked at his almost amputated right arm. At the elbow he could see bones and torn muscles and tendons ... and blood. The blood was flowing freely and quickly. He reached over with his left hand and pushed, attempting to stop the flow. When he tried to move, he found a new source of pain: two deep, four-inch lacerations to his right thigh. Dan began to yell for help.

When Dan realized no one would find him so far off the trail, he began to crawl and hobble and fall his way back down to it. That is where Chuck, Tim and Karen found him. They estimated he crawled almost one hundred yards to get back to the trail.

Chuck had some first aid training and began to assess Dan.

He realized Dan had lost a tremendous amount of blood and may need a tourniquet to stop more blood loss. Chuck began to get out his small first aid kit when the two elderly ladies arrived who had first heard Dan's cries for help.

"You can have our underwear."

"What?"

"You can have our underwear for bandages, if you need it," the ladies replied.

Tim noted they weren't wearing petticoats and for a moment felt like he had been transported back to *Gone with the Wind* when ladies offered their petticoat underwear for bandages. The thought of what underwear they were offering caught him off guard and, in the midst of this emergency, Tim found himself chuckling along with Karen. Then they heard another laugh. It was Dan's. He had found it all so very funny, for just a moment. Then Dan began to pass out as Chuck helped him onto his back. Dan needed help and he needed someone to get it for him.

With Chuck and Karen ministering to Dan, Tim became the logical choice to run for help. The nearest ranger station he knew of was fifteen miles away in the Le Conte Valley. Tim was in pretty good shape, but had just hiked up The Golden Staircase and was not a trained runner. But he had to try. From what Chuck had told him, Dan had lost a lot of blood, was losing consciousness and had shallow respirations. Tim took off his pack, turned around and began to run. It was just one o'clock in the afternoon.

Working hard to keep from twisting an ankle, Tim ran down The Golden Staircase. He didn't know how fast he was going or even how much time was passing. He did remember the pale sight of Dan and all of that blood, and that gave him the energy to keep going. But fifteen miles was a very long way and he was not optimistic about Dan's chances. Still, he kept running.

Tim estimated he had just finished mile number seven when he spotted a group of persons ahead of him. There were four in the group, three young guys and an older man. They stopped as Tim called to them and, between gulps of air, filled them in on the situation and his mission. Without hesitation, one of the tall teenagers stepped forward and volunteered to continue the run for Tim. This young man, as it turned out, was on the track team in high school. Tim quickly jotted down the information about Dan's injuries and location, and gave it to the runner who sprinted off like a deer toward the Le Conte Ranger Station eight miles away. The rest of the group headed out behind the runner with his pack as Tim turned around and started back up The Golden Staircase. Tim realized only later that he never heard the runner's name.

Sometime after 3:00 p.m., the runner made it to the Ranger Station. Ranger George and his wife, Paige, were there having just returned from an area patrol. Ranger George set the rescue in motion.

Ranger George, a Backcountry Ranger, quickly got the information from the runner. George then switched his radio channel to hit a repeater tower. Without it, no radio signals would get out of the mountains. The repeaters did just what their name implied. They received a local signal, and then sent it on its way, repeating it eventually to National Park Service Dispatch headquarters at Ash Mountain. It was 3:37 in the afternoon.

Fifteen minutes later, Lodgepole Ranger George checked to see if I was available for the medevac (short for medical evacuation). I worked primarily as a Naturalist Ranger, but when needed, used my paramedic skills to assist. I was available and quickly changed into my yellow nomex shirt and dark green pants, which are fire resistant, and my leather hiking boots. As George drove me to the helipad at Red Fir, an open area at an elevation of 6,700 feet on the forest's edge overlooking the foothills, he filled me in. He said that the call was pretty old, there was profuse bleeding, and it probably happened almost five hours ago. They hadn't received any further information. George was not optimistic and suggested I take a body bag. It was already after 4:00 p.m., and it was a long flight, almost an hour to the Southfork Pass area of Palisade Basin.

The contract pilot, Bob, and I had flown together before. The helicopter, a Bell Long Ranger, was configured for seated passengers but could quickly be changed over to accommodate a reclining patient. We put my rescue bag with intravenous (IV) fluids and bandages in with a plastic box of medications and a Miller splint board. The latter was shorter than the average board, was bright yellow and could float. It had Velcro straps to help hold a patient in place. I also put in a body bag, a thick plastic bag with a zipper that can contain body fluids, and is strong enough to be lifted intact. I hoped I wouldn't have to use it.

I always felt so fortunate when I flew. To see the whole of my beloved Sierra from such lofty heights was breathtaking. The long flight allowed me the luxury to mentally review my action plan and to sightsee. I took out the map and realized that right over the crest of the Eastern Sierra, where the patient was reported to be, were the southernmost glaciers in the United States. The Palisade Glaciers were small and tucked into the northeast-facing slopes. The Middle Palisade Glacier sat between the Thumb at 13,388 feet and Disappointment Peak at

13,917 feet. But I wouldn't be able to see the glacier as it was over the crest of the basin. The glaciers survived, in part, because they were on north-facing slopes. With the sun to the south of us as it makes its way across the sky, any south-facing slope receives a daylong bombardment of sun, and snow quickly melts with this exposure. But ice and snow on north-facing slopes are in perpetual shadow; much cooler temperatures and lack of direct sun exposure allow them to persist.

It was just after 5:00 p.m. when we made a quick landing near the Le Conte Ranger Station and picked up Backcountry Ranger George and Paige. We then took off for the basin. After climbing up the slope, we lowered into the basin in a broad arc. I could see the vast granite field dotted with occasional green shrub lines and even a bit of snow lining the higher areas below the peaks. A colorful dot came into focus as a dark green lean-to, and several persons waved up at us.

"There they are," I said.

"We've got a problem," Bob replied.

I looked over at him, even though I was hearing his voice through my headphones.

"I don't see a decent LZ near the patient; nothing is flat enough," Bob explained.

As I paid more attention to the surrounding terrain, I realized he was right. There was no area that was flat and big enough to accommodate the "footprint" landing zone, or LZ, for the helicopter. We hovered and circled and looked, but were using up time and fuel.

"Can you let me out and look some more?" I asked, as I looked him straight in the eye. His return glance told me he knew exactly what I was asking.

"You sure you want to do this?" Bob answered.

What I needed to do was get to the patient. Bob was an excellent pilot and I trusted him. There were no rules or guidelines for this kind of situation so you had to think on your feet and do the best you could with what you had. Bob knew I was asking him to hover as close to the ground as possible, and I would make my exit. We discussed it and agreed that if he could put one skid of the helicopter on a rock, he could balance it enough to keep it steady as I jumped out.

I took off my seat belt and reached back and got my rescue bag and drug box from the back seat. Bob hovered lower and lower and finally put one skid on a large white slab of granite that sloped away from the ship. It was perfect. With my helmet on, I opened the door and stepped out onto the footstep and dropped my gear. The bag skidded and rolled to a stop. I watched as the box tumbled and crashed open, spilling its contents on the rocks below through a crack in the plastic. The rotors were whirling above my head and the noise and downdraft were intimidating. I stepped down lightly onto the skid and then jumped. I focused on a particular spot just about four feet away and landed in a crouch with both feet together. I quickly moved away from the helicopter, turning to give Bob a "thumbs up" as he peeled away off the rock and into the air. "Piece of cake," I smiled to myself.

I grabbed my bag and picked up my cracked plastic box. Only a few items had spilled out and none were broken. With my helmet and nomex flight gloves still on, I made my way to the patient. The rescuers had erected a tarp of dark green with parachute cord and hiking sticks. The patient was covered with an orange tube tent and blue sleeping bag. A man in a red t-shirt stood by as a woman in a blue-and-white checkered shirt sat with the patient. It was a lot of color for one spot so far from civilization.

I was relieved to see the patient, Dan, was not only alive, but also able to talk to me. He peered out from the bundle of covers as Chuck pulled the green tarp back. Karen sat on the ground, holding Dan's left leg on her lap with the shoe off and leg elevated. It was 5:15 p.m.

As I worked on obtaining vital signs and completing my assessment, Dan, Chuck and Karen filled me in on the events from their perspective. I was able to tell them about the runner and radio relay. In wilderness medicine, you have to be able to be more aggressive with patient care, especially when you are the only medic. Since Dan was oriented, could remember all of the events of the accident, I was able to do a valid assessment of his neck. He assured me his neck did not hurt and I was able to pre-liminarily clear his cervical spine in the field. His pulse was a steady 64 beats per minute (bpm) lying down, so I sat him up briefly to see how he felt. Immediately his pulse accelerated to 110, and I laid him back down. This attempt at orthostatic vital signs (that is, pulse and blood pressure with a change in the patient's position) told me he had lost a lot of blood. Dan was also pale with moist skin, an early sign of shock. I established an IV of lactated Ringer's solution in his left arm to replace some of the lost fluids and electrolytes.

During my assessment I had seen the damage to Dan's right arm. It was partially amputated below the elbow. All of the major muscle groups had been severed as well as the radial artery. I could see the broken humerus of his upper arm and radius of his lower arm. It was a mess, but with pressure, the bleeding had stopped without a tourniquet. He could even feel his fingertips a bit.

I splinted the arm in place and covered the deep lacerations on his thigh. His left ankle was very swollen and angulated, but still had good perfusion to his toes. After splinting his ankle, I was ready to get him onto the Miller board and out of the area. Bob had managed to find a landing zone about a hundred yards away and was walking toward us with George and Paige carrying the board and oxygen. Dan's lungs were clear, but with the altitude and loss of blood, oxygen would really help his system.

As we packaged Dan onto the board, Bob confirmed our earlier plan of action. We had talked about taking the patient to an eastside hospital as needed. I felt he needed to be stabilized as soon as possible and Bob said his fuel status warranted the trip to the east. He didn't want to try to go west in the chopper on such a low tank.

Chuck and Karen helped Bob, George, Paige and me carry Dan to the helicopter, crossing the creek on the way. Bob had reconfigured the ship, opening the left side doors to the front and back and creating a bed the length of the ship. Dan told Karen and Chuck they could have anything in his pack if they could find it, and hoped they might find the camera he had dropped in the fall. Karen later said they never found the camera.

I got into the ship on the right side, belted in and secured all of my gear. I held Dan's good left hand as we took off, keeping a feel on his pulse as we climbed over the eastern crest en route to Bishop, California. I looked out to orient myself and realized, as we hit a gust at the crest, that I was looking down at the Middle Palisade Glacier. It was not large, but it was there.

We dropped into the Owens Valley and, within thirty minutes, were approaching a small airstrip where an ambulance waited. Bob told me he would refuel while I accompanied the patient.

The small hospital in Bishop was capable of stabilizing Dan, and would have normally transferred him for his delicate arm surgery. But I was told by the accepting doctor that there just happened to be a surgeon visiting for a while who was capable of reattaching Dan's arm. I was struck at Dan's luck. I later learned they successfully reattached his arm and he recovered from all of his other injuries.

The flight back over the Sierra in the helicopter was gorgeous in the late afternoon sun. We stopped to pick up Backcountry Ranger George and Paige and flew down to Grouse Meadow to drop them off. We then headed back to Red Fir. The long summer days allowed us to traverse the width of the High Sierra safely.

I looked down on all of the trails I had been on and all of the ones I wanted to take in the future. It occurred to me that, in the helicopter, I was covering the distance in minutes, rather than in the days or weeks it would take me on foot. I often thought about that on subsequent hikes when I got tired. "Oh, how I wish I had a helicopter to whisk me up this mountain," I'd muse. But then again, my life motto was: "Happiness is a journey, not a destination." I loved the getting there as much as the "there." I possessed a feeling of accomplishment when backpacking deep into the mountains. I am continually amazed at what you can do to the human body and still have it function, whether it's a grueling hike or a tragic near-fatal fall.

Second Chance

Any day I can get into the High Sierra backcountry is a good day. That is, unless I am summoned. In pre-hospital care, there are a variety of trained persons who can assist in stabilizing and transporting a patient to a healthcare facility for definitive care. There are persons with CPR (cardiopulmonary resuscitation) cards, First Aid cardholders, and First Responders.

Then there are more highly trained persons who can deliver care to the patient on scene that may be equivalent to some procedures that are done in a hospital. Emergency Medical Technicians (EMTs) come in a variety of capabilities. A Basic EMT (EMT) may have one to two hundred hours of training and can administer oxygen and maintain airways with adjuncts, among other skills. They specialize in packaging and transporting patients. Intermediate EMTs (I-EMT or Parkmedic) are able to provide some advanced life support, such as starting IVs, and administer some medications, such as epinephrine for anaphylactic shock. They undergo an additional two-hundred-plus hours of training. An EMT-Paramedic, with over one thousand hours of training, has many capabilities. They include advanced airways and EKG (electrocardiography) monitoring and interpretation. This latter skill is unique among paramedics and is very necessary when a patient shows signs and symptoms of a heart attack. On the last day of July, all of these levels would come into play to try to give someone a second chance at life.

Richard had been a Backcountry Ranger and EMT for years. In addition to patrolling the Sierra backcountry, he and others like him, assisted in coordinating projects for the backcountry. These can include cleaning up trash and clearing trails. While the work is not especially taxing, in the thin air of the backcountry, tasks are not so easily accomplished. Richard was there when a member of a volunteer group developed chest pain on the trail two miles above Hamilton Lakes.

The trail was part of the High Sierra Trail that left Crescent Meadow in Giant Forest and traversed the Sierra to Mount Whitney, seventy miles away. The spot on the trail where the patient lay was a good seventeen miles from the trailhead, over tough terrain and at about 9,000 feet above sea level. It was 10:45 a.m. and Richard immediately called for assistance.

Protection Ranger Mark and I received the call to respond and headed to the helispot at Red Fir near Lodgepole. Mark was a Parkmedic and I a paramedic. All I heard on the initial call was a seventeen-year-old male had chest pain. I was sure I had heard the age wrong, which often happens. Healthy seventeen-year-olds usually don't have heart problems. Then we received an update: the patient was unresponsive and in convulsions.

We flew past Bearpaw and Lone Pine Creek in the park contract helicopter and looked over at the massive granite formation named Valhalla. The sky was a brilliant blue which made the largest of Hamilton Lakes as blue as I had ever seen it. Surrounding the lakes was the glistening white of exposed granite and just a small amount of vegetation. We circled near the trail and saw Richard wave to us as we headed back down to the mouth of the lake. It was the only safe place to land.

There were quite a few young volunteers at the site, and after the ship shut down, they helped carry supplies up the trail to the patient. We moved out and eventually arrived at a modified lean-to in the middle of the trail with a very young-looking man – no boy – lying underneath. The picture just did not match the puzzle. I relaxed a bit when I saw it really was only a seventeen-year-old boy. It was usual for older men to have heart problems, not teenagers. Despite this, the patient looked pale and weak. I reached down and introduced myself, placing my fingers along the inside of his wrist to feel his radial pulse. Alarm bells went off as I felt a very irregular pulse run under my fingertips. He told me his name was Eddie. I could barely hear him.

I immediately turned to Mark and asked him to start an IV on Eddie for drug administration, and received a report from Richard and Gustavo. Gustavo was the counselor working with Eddie's group. Richard placed Eddie on oxygen and filled me in on his vital signs, his past medical history and medication use. Eddie was not on any medications nor had any allergies to medications. But Eddie had died before.

I placed Eddie on the heart monitor as Gustavo told me that Eddie was in a second chance program. Two years ago, at the age of fifteen, Eddie had gotten into using street drugs. In November of that year, Eddie took a combination of heroin and cocaine that stopped his heart, putting him into full arrest. They got him to a hospital and doctors there were able to revive him. The result of that was that Eddie, at fifteen, suffered a myocardial infarction (MI), a heart attack. It caused the death of some of his heart muscle and left him weak and much older than his seventeen years.

Eddie had been drug-free since that incident. He was part of a program that allowed him to give to communities through volunteer work and, in turn, feel good about himself and the life he was spared. But this day, the combination of hard work and the thin air above Hamilton Lakes probably contributed to Eddie's current heart instability.

The EKG on the heart monitor showed a premature ventricular contraction (PVC) every three to four beats. Should one of those irregular beats hit on a regular beat, it could throw the entire electrical system of the heart into chaos and no heart contractions would occur. It would just sit there and quiver like gelatin, a condition known as fibrillation. If his heart could be defibrillated quickly after onset through electrical shocks to the chest, there would be a chance of reversing fibrillation. This is the concept behind training EMTs and other first responders in the use of Automatic External Defibrillators (AEDs). I would need to calm the irregular, irritated ventricles of Eddie's heart before it fibrillated.

I gave Eddie nitroglycerin and then morphine for the chest pain as we packaged him in a litter for the carryout down the trail to the helicopter. Nitroglycerin dilates blood vessels and hopefully allows oxygenated blood to the heart muscle. It was a narrow trail and the rescuers had to take it slow to keep from falling. The chest pain continued and I kept up with the medication. I didn't have 12-lead capabilities in the field at that time, so I couldn't be positive if Eddie was having another MI. Having his electrical system screwed up was bad enough without adding heart muscle damage, too.

I was able to get out by radio through Park Dispatch to the hospital in Fresno. I received orders for administration of Lidocaine, which acts as an anesthetic to calm the heart with PVCs, but it is used in rare cases as it occasionally can cause irregular beats in the heart. We stopped on the trail while I gave Eddie a loading dose, and then piggybacked a bag of more Lidocaine to the main line. Within minutes his PVCs began to diminish in frequency and his chest pain became less and less. His lungs remained clear and he said he didn't feel quite so weak.

It took several hours to reach Eddie and get him off of the mountain, but we did. He made it to the hospital in one piece and had yet another second chance.

Laceration

I went to Everglades National Park for six months as a Park Ranger Naturalist/Interpreter. I was also a certified paramedic, but rarely used those skills. I had taken quite a bit of time to drive cross-country from California. My friend, Mary Anne, came along for fun and was set to return from Miami on our arrival. But in Marfa, Texas, she received a job offer to work at Royal Palm and accepted it. She flew back, picked up her uniform and returned. There was only one car between us, my yellow Datsun wagon that my Dad called the "yellow peril." It had so many parts replaced that I figured it was a naturalized citizen.

I wasn't very familiar with eastern toll roads and encountered a section where my Datsun, "Lemonade," (when life hands you a lemon ...) was acting up and threatening to stall. So when I threw my money in the basket at one unmanned booth, I didn't take the time to stop for a ticket because I was afraid I wouldn't get my car started again. Mary Anne commented that they would make me pay as if I had traveled the entire length of the toll road. I told her that I would just explain about Lemonade acting up. She was right … it was an expensive lesson in humanity.

I was stationed at the very tip of the Florida Peninsula at Flamingo. It was a beautiful spot, right on Florida Bay. The mangroves make islands called keys that hold a multitude of birds, including the southern Bald Eagle. On one occasion, I was driving down the road from Royal Palm, through the sawgrass prairie, past the hammocks and into the heavily vegetated area of the coastal prairie. (I love the sign on the road, with its Park Service authority proclaiming, "Rock Reef Pass, Elevation 3 Feet"!) I slowed to a crawl when I saw something in the road ahead. I was always on the lookout for wildlife and there were times when poisonous cottonmouth snakes would be coiled up on the road, some even striking at my tires. But on this occasion, there was a large bird, perhaps a turkey vulture, with its talons imbedded in a road kill. It flapped its wings in a fruitless attempt to take off, but the deceased was well-glued by the sun onto the pavement. I finally had to slow down or risk running over the bird when, to my horror, I realized it was one of the rare Bald Eagles. I stopped as I watched it repeatedly try to take off with lunch, finally leaving empty-handed.

Working as a naturalist at Flamingo was incredibly rewarding. There were so many different venues for interpretation. I gave bird walks at Eco Pond and walked into Florida Bay with a long net held by visitors that came to see what lived under the ocean's surface in my talk, "Going In Seine." I even performed as a lady pirate in a living history presentation. From walks in the sawgrass prairie to leading canoe excursions in the canals, the variety was fabulous. I especially enjoyed giving evening programs. I gave one entitled "El Lagarto," which is Spanish for "the lizard" and the origin of the word alligator.

Before the evening program, there was preparation time. I rode my bicycle from the housing area to work at the visitor center on a dirt and crushed shell path. Along the way I encountered sleeping alligators and ospreys nesting on poles. I was upstairs in the closed visitor center office, sweeping the floor, when I heard on the radio one of the Protection Rangers, Vic, say he was responding to a report of a person with a laceration down at the boat dock by the store. Vic, an Emergency Medical Technician, had just returned from a patrol with the U.S. Government boat. I distinctly remember sweeping the floor when the next radio traffic I heard was, "Nancy, get down here!"

Vic's voice was so intense that I dropped the broom, pushed the key on the radio and said, "Copy." I headed out the door. Judy, another seasonal, also headed toward the dock.

It was a short jog to the quay and I was able to look over in the light of the setting sun to see that Vic was in a speedboat that was lower than the wall of the quay. I remember it was a white boat, and as I got closer, mistook the red on top of the boat as paint … it was blood.

I grabbed some gloves from Vic's pack and asked what happened as I pulled them on and began to walk to the boat. It wasn't properly tied to the side and I reached down and grabbed a side rail to steady myself before I entered the boat. I saw a man, about twenty-nine years of age, semi-sitting on the floor of the split-level deck. I recognized him as a local man who worked for the concessionaire. It was Jack.

Vic began to tell me what little he knew. A friend of Jack's was piloting the boat in Florida Bay while Jack was "bow riding." Bow riding is sitting on the very front of the boat, or bow, with both legs dangling over the edge, the tip of the boat between them. It's a thrill ride, dangerous and illegal in Park waters.

Vic said Jack's friend was distracted by a flock of birds and didn't see the iron navigational I-beam until it was too late. The boat crashed into the beam before Jack could pull his leg out of the way. It was crushed between the boat and the unyielding iron post. Luckily, Jack fell back into the boat instead of into the bay. The driver drove as fast as he could to the harbor at Flamingo where he jumped out of the boat and yelled for help.

A woman on the quay who realized Jack was bleeding to death, jumped into the boat with a piece of polypropylene rope and tried to tie a tourniquet above the knee joint on Jack's crushed left leg. She then got out of the boat, threw up and left. We never knew the identity of the woman who tried to buy Jack some time. Ross, who worked at the Marina, saw Vic arrive and ran to get him.

I eased my way down into the boat and worked my way to Jack. I kept slipping due to the slick blood everywhere. Jack was leaning back against his sister, Linda. I lifted Jack's dangling leg and saw the horrific damage to it. Several inches below the knee, the leg was crushed. I noted a large part, about four inches of the calf muscle, was missing and assumed it was in the bay. The bones of the tibia and fibula were sheared and crushed and about three inches of muscle and fiber and skin were all that was holding the lower leg to the upper. Despite the tourniquet, the stump was still bleeding profusely. Vic was working hard to tighten the tourniquet. I called up to the gathering crowd on the dock and said I need a screwdriver. Another Park Ranger, Alan, arrived and Vic directed him to use his boat radio to request Metro Dade Fire Rescue and a helicopter.

Tourniquets are tricky and potentially dangerous things. They are used as a last resort to stop bleeding. Direct pressure and elevation are preferred, then pressure points (direct pressure on an artery above the injury). A proper tourniquet is wide and placed below joints if possible. Once in place, it should never be released in the field. Releasing a tourniquet can have several adverse effects. It can allow bleeding to restart as well as allow contaminated blood to return to the torso. Blood that has been sitting can clot and the release of blood clots or fatty tissue into the circulatory system can result in moving a clot to the lungs, a pulmonary embolism. An embolism can continue to the heart and brain and cause severe damage or death.

Though I would not have used yellow poly rope or placed it above the joint, I recognized that the unknown woman bought Jack time and, if he lived, probably kept him from bleeding to death. I didn't want to release or move it, but if it was already there and partially working, I was going to make it work more effectively.

Vic held the tourniquet while I slipped the screwdriver into a knot I created in the yellow rope and began to turn it. Jack cried out in pain as the rope bit into the flesh of his thigh. But the bleeding slowed and eventually stopped. I secured the screwdriver in place by tying it down onto the rope.

By this time another Protection Ranger, Greg, arrived with the park ambulance and asked what he could do. There was no advanced life support equipment at Flamingo at that time. The concept of cardiac intervention, intravenous fluids and field medications were still spreading throughout the parks. The Parkmedic program was not yet in place at Everglades. But we did have basic life support (BLS) capabilities. Our focus was to stabilize Jack and get him to a surgeon who, perhaps, could reattach Jack's leg.

"I need a blood pressure cuff and stethoscope, MAST pants, a cooler, ice and garbage bags … oh, and a burn blanket," I called to Greg. He tossed down a BLS bag and I opened it to see blood pressure cuff, stethoscope, penlight, trauma scissors and bandages. A quick check of Jack's vital signs was not promising. His systolic blood pressure was only 82 when it should have been 120, and his pulse of 120 was weak and thready under my fingers. He was pale, cool and clammy and had lost a lot of blood. I completed a quick survey to make sure he wasn't hurt anywhere else. He said he was a bit dizzy, but answered all of my questions appropriately. We put him in shock position to help his blood pressure.

"How long before the helicopter arrives?" I called up.

Judy said she would check on an estimated time of arrival (ETA) for the helicopter. Vic stayed with the tourniquet and continued to control the bleeding.

"We need to get him out of here and onto the dock. Can someone get this railing out of the way?" I asked.

Almost instantly, several sets of strong hands reached over and literally ripped the side rail right off the boat. I paused in disbelief at the show of strength. There was a lot of adrenaline flowing that day. I saw several people I knew up there: Larry, a Park Service employee as well as many local fishermen.

I needed to get Jack out of the boat and into MAST trousers. I was hoping it would stabilize his leg and had anecdotal information of them working in patients who were bleeding out.

A man was lowered down in the now secured boat. I didn't recognize him.

He was about middle-age and just stood behind me. I turned my attention to Jack.

"Look, Jack, you have seen your leg and what happened to it, haven't you?" I started. Jack nodded.

"If there is any chance of preserving it so it can be reattached, we have to put it on ice. We want to put a pneumatic anti-shock garment on you to help stabilize you because we don't have IV fluids available. I need to buy you some more time."

Again, Jack nodded, but I wasn't sure I was getting through to him. My next statement did.

"Jack, I have to cut your leg off," I said.

He stared right back at me, and said only two words: "Do it."

I reached down to pick up the trauma scissors from the BLS bag and bumped into the man behind me. I turned to him briefly and said, "Who are you?"

"I'm James. I'm a doctor and came to see if I can help," he said.

"What kind of doctor?" I asked.

"A surgeon," he replied.

Happy days, I thought.

"Well, you heard what I said to Jack; do you agree?" I asked James.

"Totally. Go right ahead, you're doing fine," he replied.

Fine, I thought.

"Don't you want to perform the amputation?" I asked.

"You're doing fine. Go right ahead," he replied.

I was not about to get into any kind of a discussion, so I said, "Okay, I will need you to bandage the stump. The dressings are in there," I motioned to the BLS bag.

I turned back to Ranger Greg. "Ready with the blanket, Greg, his leg is coming to you. Blanket, bag and then on ice," I called up.

"Ready," Greg answered.

I turned to Jack and said, "This will probably hurt. I don't have any morphine and, even if I did, your blood pressure is too low. Bite down on this," I said. I reached over and placed the empty blood pressure case between Jack's teeth and he clamped down on it. His sister continued to give him physical and mental support.

I held Jack's lower leg by the splintered bones and little flesh left on his calf with my left arm and hand and pinched it under my armpit. Vic supported Jack's thigh. I took the silver-bladed trauma scissors with the black handles in my right hand and opened the blades to the muscle and skin still attached to Jack. Then I began to cut. I cut and cut and cut, repeatedly and as fast as I could. Jack squirmed a little and let go with a moan, but that was it. Within seconds I was through. I picked up his leg by the big toe and the calf area and reached up toward Greg. Holding a man's detached leg by the big toe and moving it free of the man is a sobering experience. There were gasps from the surrounding crowd as I placed it in the sterile burn blanket Greg held. He wrapped it carefully, placed it in clean garbage bags and then into the cooler. We didn't want to frostbite the leg by putting it directly on ice and wanted to eliminate as much contamination to the limb as possible.

James and I quickly bandaged the stump. We lifted Jack out of the boat to waiting hands. The EMTs on the dock placed Jack in the MAST pants, on the backboard and gurney, gave him oxygen and placed him into the ambulance with Alan and Vic. Just then, I heard the massive whirr of the Coast Guard helicopter as it descended into Flamingo from the north. The ambulance pulled out with Jack and several EMTs on board as I was assisted out of the boat. In the dusk we watched as the huge red and white ship began to lower onto the grassy area in front of the visitor center. Then we all held our breath as we realized it was heading right for the flagpole! A combination of expert ground marshalling and radio work averted a disaster and the chopper landed safely. Within minutes, a Coast Guard paramedic had started an IV on Jack. He was taken on board and the helicopter lifted off to Mercy Hospital in Miami, with Jack and his leg on ice.

I pulled off my gloves and asked the time. I had fifteen minutes before my program. The Protection Rangers all offered to clean up so I could still make my event. I thanked them and jogged off to the campfire circle on the shore in the campground.

By this time it was dark and I was able to take a minute to compose myself and to answer questions that are the norm before the formal program. The presentation on alligators came off without a hitch and I stayed around to answer more questions in the dim light of the amphitheater.

After the last person left, I gathered my slide tray and returned to the visitor center. I put the tray in its slot and looked down at my arms. My gray long-sleeved uniform shirt was wet with blood from the cuffs to the upper arms. I hadn't noticed it at all in the dark of the evening program and, thank goodness, none of the visitors did either. What a gruesome turn of events that would have been.

I rolled up my sleeves and washed the blood off of my fore-arms. Then I went back downstairs, unlocked my bike and rode back to the housing area. As I rode down the row of trailers, I noticed an odd thing. People were outside. That was unusual in the mosquito-thick evenings of the Everglades. When I got closer, they began to crowd around me. I got off and walked my bike and my neighbors and coworkers all began to clap. I was flabbergasted. Then they complimented me on my assistance to Jack and how great it was that he made it.

"He did?" I asked.

They all answered in the affirmative. He had gotten to the hospital alive.

Epilogue

I visited Jack a few days later in Mercy Hospital in Miami. He was in excellent spirits, despite the fact that they were not able to reattach his leg. Too much had fallen into Florida Bay during the accident.

Jack was fitted with an artificial leg and, a few months later, sent a letter telling me all about the backpacking trip he was planning in his future.

The Plan

■ Death Valley, California

The visitation in Death Valley really grows in the wintertime. Not that people don't come in the summer. In July and August folks from all over the world rent cars in Las Vegas and drive the two to three hours to the Furnace Creek visitor center located below sea level. They open the doors of their air-conditioned cars and practically fall on the pavement when the 120-degree heat hits them full force. So most prefer to visit in the winter months of November through March.

Death Valley had some interesting jurisdictional issues. There was a donut-hole of private land, the Furnace Creek Ranch that was protected by the Inyo County Sheriff's Office (ICSO). ICSO often took the lead on major felonies on Park Service lands. Next to the ranch was a small patch of Timbisha Tribal land. The California Highway Patrol took charge of the main highway, and the National Park Service went to all of these areas with some limitations in their authority, but always with mutual aid in mind.

The staffing was very limited following the holidays and, on

January 2, I found I was only one of two Protection Rangers on duty in the Furnace Creek area. As a Protection Ranger, I was responsible for law enforcement, search and rescue, emergency medical services and structural fire. It was a one-stop-shopping job, but I loved the variety and never knew what would happen next. Sometimes there were long periods of quiet punctuated with short periods of chaos.

I had just walked into my residence at Cow Creek, a few miles from the Visitor Center/Headquarters when my radio call number was put on the air. Karen, one of the Ranger Naturalists, asked if I could come to the visitor center. She stated, in an agitated voice, that a man just walked in and said he was committing suicide! I dashed to my marked patrol vehicle, a Ford Bronco, and sped down the hill to the highway. I asked Karen if there were any weapons involved and she said she couldn't see any. I arrived in minutes, ran to the front door of the visitor center, then entered. Karen motioned to the supervisor's office to the side and said, "He's in there." I cautiously looked through the open door of the office to see a nervous middle-aged man sitting down with another Protection Ranger, Greg. Greg, who worked up at Scottys Castle, had arrived just before me and was with the gentlemen, waiting for my arrival. I went back to Karen to try to figure out what was going on.

"I don't understand, I thought you said he was trying to kill himself?"

Karen explained that this man came in and reported that his vehicle had been involved in a car accident. Karen called for a ranger and Greg offered to take the accident report before returning to the castle as he heard me just break for lunch. While waiting for Ranger Greg, the man turned to Karen, pulled down his t-shirt and exposed a bleeding laceration that went across his neck and said, "I tried to kill myself." The blood and announcement startled her so that Karen put the radio call out as if it were happening that very moment.

I entered the room and introduced myself. I eyed Greg who was in a defensive posture. The man said his name was Leo. He was agitated, with a short attention span. I conducted a search for weapons on Leo with Greg watching intently. Leo had a charcoal-like residue on his clothing and smelled of fire. He had no identification, just over $7.00 and two rocks in his pants pockets. In his left breast pocket he had a Remington PMC .223 caliber bullet. I then asked Leo to sit down and told him I was also a paramedic. I asked to look at his neck wound. Leo had a thin laceration with dried blood extending from below his right ear to just short of his left ear. I offered to clean it up for him but he became almost manic in his behavior and started to mumble. Greg took a step forward and I let Leo's shirt go and stepped back. I calmly assured him that we could take care of his "cut" another time and that seemed to soothe him.

I walked over to Greg and said, "This guy's a 5150." Greg lifted his eyebrows in agreement as if to say, "No kidding." The California legal statute, which in part has the last numbers "5150" is often referred to as the psych or endangerment statute. If a person is a danger to himself or to others, or is gravely disabled, he/she can be taken against his/her will for a psychiatric hold for treatment of physical or mental illness. As an extension, "5150" became slang for anyone we wanted to call crazy or psychologically disturbed without them knowing it. This was an Inyo County case as county deputies could impose the California statute while rangers in Death Valley could not. At that time,

Park Rangers did not assimilate that code among the federal laws they enforced.

Leaving the door open, Greg went to a phone outside of the office to call for the Inyo County Sheriff Deputy while still keeping an eye on the two of us. I pulled up a chair, keeping a corner of the desk between us, and Leo's back to the partially open door. I wanted him to calm down, but I didn't want to compromise my safety while trying to communicate with him. I also didn't want to escalate the situation by agitating Leo. I reached out and put my hand on his knee and said, "Leo, tell me what happened." He burst into tears and then quieted down. I kept my hand on him as I looked up to see Greg put up two fingers and mouth the words, "Two hours." That meant that the resident deputy, Don, was out of the area and another deputy would have to drive to the valley from Lone Pine. I took a deep sigh and settled in with Leo as Greg took up residence outside the room.

Leo said that seven years ago he had lost his job. He had worked with older mainframe computers, but there wasn't much call for that expertise in the era of mini-computers. He tried unemployment for a few months, but then a series of personal tragedies occurred. His brother-in-law died, then his father and then his brother, all within weeks of each other. The stress caused him to develop tinnitus, a ringing in his ears that never went away. As life got progressively worse, Leo made a decision. He made a plan.

Leo decided he would live off of his savings of about $50,000, and then "terminate" himself. He calculated he had enough money to last seven years. In that time, he rarely answered the phone and spent his time reading and working on his Mac computer. He severed his family ties, settled his lease and paid off all his bills.

This past December 16, with the last of his money, he left his home on the coast with his few remaining belongings. He went to the ocean, threw his computer and over three hundred disks of software into the water, and headed to Hoover Dam by a long and circuitous route. There, he planned to drive off the dam and end his life. But when he got to the dam there was so much construction, he couldn't find any access to the edge and had to change his plan. Leo took out a map and saw the name, Death Valley, and knew that was where he was to die. On December 30, Leo drove his white van to Beatty, Nevada, one of the gateway towns to Death Valley, and bought some food. He then drove toward the valley and camped on the road entrance to Titus Canyon.

Titus Canyon is spectacular, with a twisting meandering dirt road that requires high clearance vehicles and often four-wheel drive. Views from the red rock at Bloody Gap and the storied history of Leadville are complemented by the geologic spectacle of twisted rocks. Bighorn sheep and ancient petroglyphs can be seen by the quiet and adventurous who get out of their cars during the drive.

On December 31, New Year's Eve, Leo had a very specific plan for his death that he called his "termination plan." He removed all of his identification and took off his vehicle license plate. He broke this into pieces and buried it. His plan had several complicated components to assure his death. At 6:00 p.m., he drove to the edge of a cliff in Titus and sat there until midnight. He planned to drive over the cliff, and taped a screwdriver to the steering wheel to impale himself in the chest on impact. He poured gasoline throughout the van to start a fire and placed a bullet in his left front pocket so it would explode and "blow his heart out" in the fire. He tied piano wire around his neck and fastened the ends to each of the driver and passenger doorframes to garrote himself in the fall.

At midnight, Leo started gasoline-soaked rags on fire, threw them into the back of the van and drove off the cliff. In the dark he did not see that there was a landing only fifteen feet below. The wire cut his neck, but he was not impaled because his seat belt prevented it. He wore it because he didn't want to be thrown from the van and possibly saved from the fire. He wanted all of him and who he was to be destroyed.

After the van stopped on the landing, Leo realized he had survived the fall. By this time, the van was becoming fully engulfed in flames and it wasn't in his plan to be burned alive. So he released his seat belt and scurried back up to the road and watched his van burn completely. As he sat there all night, Leo said he thought of jumping off another cliff, but had trouble formulating this concept because it wasn't a part of the termination plan he had so carefully crafted. At daylight, Leo began walking through Titus Canyon. Soon a visitor, Forrest, came by in a white pickup truck. Leo told him he had car problems so Forrest gave Leo a ride to the visitor center. When I asked Leo if he told Forrest he had tried to kill himself, Leo said he didn't because it wasn't part of his plan.

Leo finally let me clean up his neck wound and, at 2:00 p.m., Deputy Paul arrived. I switched places with Greg and filled Paul in on Leo's life and termination plan. Paul looked at me obliquely and asked if I could write it up. I wrote some quick notes and gave them to Paul who placed Leo into handcuffs after searching him again. This was to insure the deputy's safety during transport. At 3:40 p.m., Leo was taken out the back door to the employee lot and placed into the deputy's patrol car. Before Paul closed the door, I heard Leo mumbling to himself about how he needed a "new plan."

Death Valley Dates

I was the only Protection Ranger on duty in Stovepipe Wells that day. I was a seasonal and one of the two permanent rangers had transferred out recently. There were campground hosts and volunteers I had worked with to collect the campground fees, drive the ambulance, and work the radio in case someone needed me when I was out of the developed area. In almost a million acres of land there was only one other Protection Ranger in the vicinity. She, too, was named Nancy, was also a paramedic and had attended seasonal law enforcement academy with me. In fact, one of the nicest Thanksgivings I ever spent was up in Nancy's assigned area of Wildrose. It was a welcome change for me to be in the mountains with the incredibly gorgeous scenery. Unlike the sea level sand dunes and desert of Stovepipe Wells, Wildrose, at over 5,000 feet, had pinyon pines, narrow canyons and green shrubbery.

Nancy was truly the lone ranger up there. There were no phones and I was her closest backup, forty-five minutes away. Once, she single-handedly arrested two car thieves who stopped for gas after getting lost.

By February, things were really picking up in Death Valley. The day before, a local Stovepipe Wells resident had an irregular heart rate. We called for a life flight helicopter out of Las Vegas, the nearest town that had hospitals and doctors. By ground ambulance, it was a three-hour one-way drive to Las Vegas, but only two hours round trip for a helicopter to come from Las Vegas, pick up the patient and have them return to a hospital there. An hour can make a huge difference in a critical patient.

The next day I worked a busy but uneventful shift in the Stovepipe Wells area. The sun set early in the winter and I got off of work after 5:30 p.m. I retreated to my government trailer with its familiar generic oak furniture and had a snack. Then I jumped on my exercise bicycle for a vigorous workout. Although I preferred to run, it was too dark and the rocky road would almost guarantee a twisted ankle. A little after 6:00 p.m., my park radio began to crackle. That was unusual because I almost always turned it off and put it in the charger to avoid a dead battery should I be called out. I am usually called by telephone for emergencies after hours and don't really need the radio. I got off the bike and was about to turn it off when I heard my name. That was really peculiar as I had an assigned call number. We rarely use names on the radio, preferring numbers that indicate area assignments and order of rank.

"Nancy are you there?" a faint voice called.

I immediately recognized Ranger Nancy up at Wildrose. Her voice sounded weak and in pain. I answered, asking if she was okay. She said she thought so, but wondered if I could come up and help her with a "situation." There were no phones at

Wildrose so this was the only way Nancy could call for help.

I read between the lines that she was asking for medical help. A week ago, her husband-to-be, Joe, had taken her to the hospital for a painful kidney stone. I have never experienced a kidney stone but I have treated many patients with them. Imagine a piece of cinder in the palm of your hand and someone stepping on it, grinding it in. That was one patient's description. Rarely life threatening, the pain is excruciating and the patient can become incapacitated. Because the muscular action of the ureter (the tube between the kidney and the bladder) squeezes and relaxes, the pain increases and decreases, causing patients to be agitated, wanting to walk around and often vomit when they are not doubled over in pain.

I asked Nancy on the radio if she thought it was the same thing as last week. I was loath to ask her on the air if it was another kidney stone. There were lots of people with scanners and I tried to keep her personal details private. Again she answered weakly that she thought so. I was puzzled. Nancy is a strong and incredibly capable ranger, and I could tell by her voice that she hurt, but I wasn't sure how badly. I didn't want to over-react, but I wasn't getting a sense from her of how bad she was. For most kidney stones, a narcotic like Demerol or morphine will do the trick until the pain subsides. The stone can then be passed and the event is over.

"Nancy, do you want an ambulance or just medication?" I radioed. She said she thought just the meds, as we call them, were all she needed. There were only a handful of medics in the more than two million acres of Death Valley. We all carried an advanced life support (ALS) bag with advanced airways, IV fluids and an assortment of prehospital care medications. We could help in an asthma attack, trauma, or heart attack while waiting for an ambulance to come, which usually took quite a while.

I had trained some volunteers at Stovepipe Wells to drive our old ambulance. I knew it ran rough and was slow, especially going up the road to Wildrose, so I quickly contacted a volunteer and asked them to stand by a radio in case I needed the ambulance. I gathered my gear together and started the long drive into the Panamint Mountains. I was on the road within five minutes of Nancy's call. My patrol car had a light bar, good engine and a lot of speed, even up hills. I wanted to ease her agony in less than the forty-five minutes it usually took me to get there. My car is as multipurpose as my job. In addition to being a medic, I am also a structural firefighter, search and rescue specialist and Federal Law Enforcement Officer. To safely transport arrested persons to jail and to court, there was a metal cage between the front and back seat of my sedan. This prevented suspects from harming the officer in front, should they try.

We didn't have a dispatch center in Death Valley, so we relied on phones and rangers keeping their radios on. As I drove up the road to Emigrant Junction, I called Nancy, assuring her that I was on my way. She responded, weaker than ever, saying that she felt worse and was in more pain. I stepped it up, but was taken aback by her next message.

"Nanc, I think I am going to pass out."

All of my suppositions of what was wrong with her went right out the window. Kidney stone patients don't pass out, as much as they would like to. I immediately knew something else was wrong and my sixth sense said it was serious. I told her to hang on, that I was coming code-3 and was requesting an ambulance. I knew she was really in trouble when she didn't object. I tried calling my volunteer at Stovepipe Wells to start up the hill with the ambulance. Before I heard from him, the Chief Ranger, Dale, said he would get one going my way. He had been monitoring the radio and was abreast of the situation. My surprise came when I heard Ranger Dan, from Scottys Castle thirty-five miles to the north, come in service and head toward Stovepipe for the ambulance. I didn't have time to worry about what had happened to the Stovepipe volunteer. I was now past the junction and headed to Wildrose. I went from a steep but straight road to one of the windiest paved roads in the park. One section is even called the rattlesnake for the repeated curves in the road. During my seasonal law enforcement training at Santa Rosa, California, we went to Sears Point to the Bob Bondurant Law Enforcement Driving Academy. All that I learned really paid off on this drive. I pulled up to the walkway to Nancy's small bungalow in thirty-seven minutes.

I grabbed my ALS bag and oxygen and trotted the fifty feet to her door. I always knew when I was at Nancy's. Her dog, Wiley, a Border Collie mix, was barking his head off at the screen door. I called her name and pushed the door open. There was Nancy, white as a sheet, wet with sweat and lying on the floor.

I said, "Nancy, I'm here. How are you?" And I knew right away she was bleeding to death.

I had seen this presentation in other patients. As a patient loses blood, there is less to circulate in the body. The body responds to the emergency by shutting down unnecessary blood flow to the arms and legs and skin, giving a patient a pale appearance. This also results in skin cold to the touch. The release of adrenaline (epinephrine) causes the body to sweat, makes the heart beat faster to compensate, and tries to keep the blood pressure as normal as possible for as long as it can. Normal pulse is about 80 beats per minute and blood pressure 120/80 mm Hg. In a compromised patient, a rise in pulse of more than 20 beats per minute or a drop in systolic pressure (the upper number) of 20 points shows the body is trying to compensate for the loss of blood.

I knelt next to her head and felt the weak, thready pulse in her wrist at well over 100.

"Nancy, I think you are bleeding internally."

Without hesitation she said, "I think so, too."

I was in the middle of nowhere with little communication and little help. I needed a helicopter. But first, Nancy had to be stabilized. I had only one tank of oxygen and had to make it last. Normally I would have given Nancy 15 liters per minute (lpm) of pure oxygen with a non-rebreather mask. Air is 21% oxygen. In a rebreather, a mask with a reservoir bag attached, I could approach 95% oxygen delivery, but my tank would be empty in ten to fifteen minutes at that rate. So I put her on a nasal cannula at 6 lpm. While I did this, Wiley was literally jumping all over me. Nancy's weak voice was imploring him to "get down," but I could barely hear her, nor could Wiley. I jumped up off of my knees, grabbed him by the collar and dragged him across the wooden floor to her bedroom. With an extra bit of strength, I slid him into the room and closed the door before he hit it full force on the return.

An average person has about six liters of blood circulating in their body. Despite Nancy's competence, she was smaller than average. I needed to help what little blood was in her system to circulate so the red blood cells could continue their job of delivering oxygen and picking up carbon dioxide as waste gas.

The brain and the heart needed oxygen the most. If those organs fail, the patient fails. If you take everything out of blood except water and salt, you have 0.9% normal saline. That was the IV fluid I was setting up to establish in one of Nancy's veins. I needed to use a large catheter, which is a needle with a plastic tube over it. The needle is used to pierce the skin, the catheter is slid into the vein and the needle removed. A large catheter is an 18-gauge and a 16-gauge is larger still. The larger the catheter I could get in, the faster the fluids could enter the system to try to stem the tide of exsanguination or bleeding out. The only problem is that a patient who is bleeding severely as Nancy was, usually has few surface veins due to the body's response of shutting down all but the essential vessels of the circulatory system.

As I set up my IV, I asked Nancy questions. What medications was she on, what was her past medical history, was there any recent trauma? She had a medic alert tag showing she was allergic to bees and, apart from her kidney stone, was otherwise healthy. She told me she was nauseous and that her pain was an "8" on a 1-10 scale. I then asked the question that gave me the answer to her critical situation.

"When was your last menstrual period?"

She replied that her period was late by two weeks but that she was on birth control pills. With that answer, I was sure Nancy had a ruptured ectopic pregnancy and that the clock was ticking ... very loudly. Despite the use of birth control pills, pregnancies can happen. Under normal circumstances, an egg or ovum is released by a woman's ovary and starts its journey toward the uterus through the fallopian tube. Fertilization of the ovum takes place in the tube. Sperm has traveled all the way through the uterus into the tube on its determined mission. The fertilized egg normally makes its way through the rest of the tube and implants itself in the uterus where it grows hugely over the next weeks and months to become a newborn baby nine months later. In an ectopic pregnancy, the fertilized egg plants somewhere outside the uterus, often in the fallopian tube where it was inseminated. It finds a blood vessel to tap into and begins its tremendous rate of growth. But fallopian tubes are small and narrow, not capable of expanding like the uterus. As the fertilized egg divides and grows, in just a few short weeks it's much too large for the tube. The tube bursts, rupturing the blood supply and spilling blood into the body cavity. Blood in the abdominal cavity is a great irritant and causes a lot of pain. Nancy was in a lot of pain now, but was fooled early on by thinking it was a return of a kidney stone problem. When I assessed her abdomen, I found it distended and tight and Nancy stiffened with pain as I touched her abdomen as gently as I could. Her abdominal cavity was filling up with blood.

I knelt down on her right side and placed a tourniquet on Nancy's arm to try to pool blood in her veins. She was very cold and pale, but she was athletic, so I could see the outline of a vein under the skin of her right arm opposite the elbow ... the antecubital site or AC. With a 16-gauge catheter, I was able to establish the IV of normal saline and opened the bag wide open after releasing the tourniquet. I set the bag on the table to the side and spoke to Nancy as I covered her with a quilt I found in the room and put her in shock position by lifting her feet onto my ALS bag. I tried to use my portable radio but I couldn't reach anyone from her house.

"Nancy, you're going to be fine. You look pretty stable," I lied, "but I don't want to take any chances. I am going to call for a helicopter and get help. I have to leave you for just a few minutes but I will be back. I promise."

She weakly smiled and nodded her head that she understood. I raced out the door to my vehicle radio. I got hold of Ranger Dale right away and told him I had a patient in severe shock from probable blood loss and needed a chopper. He said he would get right on it. I then ran in the dark, down the road to a small house that looked more like a shack. In it was another man named Dale, a volunteer who helped out at Wildrose now and again. I prayed that he would be home.

I pounded on the door and yelled, "Dale, Dale!"

A startled Volunteer Dale came to the door in boxers and a t-shirt. I told him there was an emergency and that I needed him up at Nancy's house right away. With few words, he turned to dress and put on some shoes. I ran back to my car to ask if there was any way a helicopter could land at Wildrose. I already knew the answer. With the steep cliffs and small trees in the dark night, there was no way. I was told the nearest LZ was probably the airport at Stovepipe Wells, but perhaps the ship could land at Emigrant Junction if we got there at the same time. I then asked the status of the ambulance. I was told that Dan and EMT Maya were in the vicinity of Stovepipe Wells. I knew I had to cut the time down and meet them part way and that meant putting Nancy in my patrol car. I opened the back door of my car, turned on the dome light and ran back into the house.

I went from frenetic to calm in a millisecond. I told Nancy a ship was coming but it would be down at Emigrant or Stovepipe and that we would meet the ambulance partway. I pulled out my blood pressure (BP) cuff and she was still compensating well: 120/62 but a pulse of 104 and respirations of twenty per minute.

Volunteer Dale arrived and I told him I needed him to help me carry Nancy to the back of my car. We placed her on the quilt with the oxygen tank and liter of normal saline attached to the IV in her arm and lifted her off of the floor. In the dark, we staggered a bit with the unwieldy load, but got her to the car. Dale held her up as I went to the other side and pulled her through on the quilt. I used a hemostat to attach the IV bag to the grating of the arrest cage. I asked Dale to go back in and get my ALS bag just as Nancy called out, "Wiley."

I said, "He is in your room and will be okay."

She said she wanted him, even though I assured her he would be fine, that Dale would look after him. With newfound strength and increasing agitation, Nancy's voice got even louder and she declared, "I'm not leaving without Wiley."

Now I know that one of the first signs of lack of oxygen to the brain is agitation and often combativeness. I had no time to waste and knew I could never reason with a hypoxic (low oxygen) Nancy. I was afraid her agitation would increase and her heart would pump even faster. I gave in. As Dale placed my ALS bag on the floor of the front seat of my vehicle, I raced back into the house, burst into the bedroom, scooped Wiley into my arms and ran back to the car. I practically threw him into my side of the car and scooted him across to the passenger side. Nancy instantly became calmer.

I went into the back seat and talked to her briefly, trying to keep her thoughts with me.

"Okay Nancy, what rate should that fluid be going in?"

"Wide open," she replied.

I took her right hand and had her wrap it around the bag.

"I need you to give yourself a fluid challenge, so squeeze the bag as much as you can." I was amazed to see her do just that. By squeezing the bag the fluid goes in more quickly, challenging the system with a lot of fluid in a short time in an effort to keep the circulatory system from collapsing.

With a wave of thanks to Dale, I jumped in my patrol car and headed back down the mountain. I left the dome light on so I could keep an eye on Nancy. This had the added benefit of seeing Wiley to my right and his reflection in the front passenger window. He was panting away and starting to steam things up so I cracked the window and he stuck the tip of his nose out. Apparently Wiley loved to go for rides.

I got on my radio and made contact with Dan and Maya in the ambulance. They told me where they were and would try to find a level straight stretch of road as we got closer. They confirmed that a life flight helicopter from Las Vegas was on its way.

I continued to talk to Nancy to make sure she was still with me. I peered in my rear view mirror but could only see her hand on the bag of normal saline. I couldn't believe she was strong enough to still have a grip.

Past the turnoff to Skidoo, I saw the ambulance. Dan had turned it around facing downhill and Maya had everything ready for us. A backboard on the gurney, the MAST pants open on the backboard and a second bag of normal saline spiked and ready to go. The timing was perfect.

I pulled up behind the ambulance and we gingerly pulled Nancy from the back of the patrol car and onto the backboard. As Dan and Maya wheeled the gurney to the ambulance, I looked right at Wiley and told him it was the end of the ride for him. I left the dome light on, turned on the music radio and locked the patrol car doors with Wiley inside. What a sight that must have been for anyone who may have driven by. Luckily, Nancy didn't insist that Wiley accompany us. The fact that she didn't notice caused me concern.

Dan got in the front and started the drive to Stovepipe Wells airport. In the back of the ambulance, we placed the MAST pants on Nancy. Maya inflated the legs while I started a second large-bore IV in her left AC. Maya placed Nancy on high flow oxygen, fifteen liters by non-rebreather while I worked on getting vital signs and placing her on the heart monitor. Nancy told me she didn't feel right. She said she felt like she was "going away." That really scared me. When patients express feelings of impending doom, they are almost always right.

I kept quizzing her. "Okay Nanc, what line should I start, what size catheter, what rate would you pick?" She was sluggish and barely audible but answered everything correctly. I could not believe she was still coherent, let alone conscious. The vital signs were showing deterioration: BP 100/60, pulse 108. Then the systolic, the upper number, dropped into the 90s. It was 7:20 p.m., just over an hour since I received the initial call. I replaced the first bag of normal saline, which was now empty, with another full liter. We broke the seal on heat packs by stomping on them, allowing the chemicals to merge and create heat. We wrapped the IV lines around the warm bags to increase the temperature of the IV fluids going in. Nancy started to complain of the cold. She also asked about her vital signs. I told her they were stable and strong and made up a number to keep her from knowing that she was really in trouble. This seemed to calm her.

We broke more heat packs and put them on her thermal windows, which are places in the body where arteries are close to the skin and could pick up the warmth. They are the armpits and the groin, places most of us unwittingly know about already as we put our hands there to warm them up when cold. We put hot packs on her chest and under her neck, covered her with blankets and cranked up the heat. Within minutes Maya and I were sweating bullets and stripping off jackets and vests. Still Nancy shivered. I took her BP again by palpation. In a moving ambulance it is hard to hear through a stethoscope, so after the blood pressure cuff is inflated, the systolic pressure is detected when the medic's fingers feel the pulse in the radial artery on the wrist. It was 90/p (p for palpation). I pulled the blankets back and was horrified to see Nancy's abdomen so distended, she looked eight months pregnant! I retook her pressure and now it was 80/p with a capillary refill of 3.5 seconds in her fingertips. (Capillary refill is the measure of perfusion or blood circulation. It is normally less than two seconds).

I had to inflate the rest of the MAST pants. What I needed most now was help in slowing or stopping Nancy's internal bleeding. She needed a surgeon, and we were trying to get her to one, but we were running out of time. I needed pressure on the bleeder inside. If this bleeder were on an arm, I'd use a pad and put direct pressure on the vessel to stop the bleeding. I couldn't reach this bleeder. I needed to inflate the abdominal compartment of the MAST to try to tamponade or stop the bleeding by putting pressure on the fluids and organs in her abdomen. We checked to be sure the abdominal segment was below her rib cage so it would not inhibit her respirations, which were now 28 per minute. Then we started to pump up the abdominal compartment. Nancy cried out in pain and pushed out at us. She was trying to fight the pain by pushing us and our pressure away. I explained to her that we had to get a handle on this before her blood pressure got too low. I never told her her real pressure. I didn't want to feed the doom she was already feeling. After we inflated the MAST pants, the pressure caused an evacuation of Nancy's bowels. She tried to apologize as the smell of stool filled the ambulance compartment. Maya and I simply cracked a window, reassured Nancy that it was just "us gals here," and proceeded to clean up the diarrhea mess.

As we rounded the corner at Emigrant Junction I could hear the traffic from the life flight helicopter. A familiar voice, an RN named Kathy, was saying something. Then, I heard more radio traffic and Dan got on the radio. It was only eight miles now to the LZ and I felt, for the first time, that Nancy would make it.

Dan called back through the opening between the driver compartment and the patient care area. I stuck my head in close to his and could see the lights of Stovepipe Wells in the distance and what I thought was the light of the helicopter beyond in the darkness. I couldn't quite make it out, as it was getting smaller and smaller.

"They're turning back," Dan said.

I was shocked.

"What?"

"They're turning back, the pilot can't land. He has vertigo and can't land because of the elevation change. He has vertigo."

"No ... no, no, no, no ... they have to, Dan. She won't make it otherwise," I blurted out.

I could hear the angst in his voice and the helpless feeling that swept over the two of us. If he could, he would have reached out and pulled the ship to the ground but he couldn't.

"Keep going," I said.

"What?" Dan replied.

"Keep going; keep going to Furnace Creek airport. Get me another chopper. Be very clear, Dan. Tell them she will die without a helicopter."

I went to the back and quietly explained the situation to Maya. The shock on her face was ephemeral. She got right back to treating Nancy as if nothing had changed.

"Nancy, a slight change of plans. We are going a bit further to pick up the chopper – just on to Furnace Creek. It's the smart thing to close the distance and cut down the travel time for it."

Furnace Creek was another thirty miles away. I had no idea if she would make it.

But her pressure came up a bit, 84/p. At least it wasn't falling anymore. And as it stabilized, her pulse climbed to 114, then to 120. We pushed more IV fluids, added more hot packs and kept monitoring her. On the downhill stretch, toward Furnace Creek, we dropped below sea level and Dan called out that another chopper was on the way.

The amazing thing at this point was that Nancy was still awake. I had no idea how, but she was, barely. We arrived at the Furnace Creek airport and waited. I felt people outside the ambulance lean against it to talk to Dan or peer inside. I asked Dan to ask people not to touch the ambulance. I was so afraid any little jostle would undo the tamponade we were apparently able to achieve. Here she had just had one hell of an ambulance ride and I was worried about a little jostle. I just had this sense that Nancy was barely with us. I didn't want to lose the little that was left.

It seemed like a long time before I finally heard the familiar whirr of a chopper as it approached and landed. We gently unloaded Nancy and took her to the medic on board. I gave a quick report, holding Nancy's hand the whole time. With the smallest of grips she squeezed my hand and whispered, "Don't go." My heart fell. I didn't know if I would ever see her again. I looked right into her eyes and said, "You will be fine. I will be there. You will make it." She then asked me to tell Joe and her parents she loved them. This sent a chill up my spine, so I said sure, squeezed her hand and stepped back as they completed closing up the ship's door and took off into the night.

My goodness it was quiet. I turned around and was blinded by the lights of the ambulance. Maya and I gave each other a hug, and then hugged Dan. None of us could say a thing. I think we were afraid to say out loud what we really felt.

Chief Ranger Dale walked up to me and said, "Go."

I was confused.

"Go where?" I asked.

"To Las Vegas," he replied.

I couldn't believe he was saying that. It's exactly what I wanted to do and where I wanted to be.

"But my car is at Stovepipe with everything, and Wiley!" I only just remembered.

Arrangements had already been made to rescue Wiley and my patrol car. Wiley had been taken to a family at Stovepipe Wells who also had a dog. My patrol car would soon be here and Dale told me to use it to go, stay at any hotel and save the receipts. He said I would be reimbursed and that no matter the outcome, I had done a good job. I was grateful for his words, but I wanted only one outcome. I also wanted to help clean the ambulance, but it was being done as a group effort by all the friends at Furnace Creek who had waited at the airport.

When my patrol car arrived, I jumped in and drove all the

way back to Stovepipe Wells. I took the time to repack my ALS bag. There is some sort of curse that if you don't repack it you are sure to get another call immediately and will be unprepared. I changed quickly and headed up over Daylight Pass to Beatty, Nevada, and onto Highway 95 to Vegas. I am a pretty conservative driver, but I really opened it up on my way in and made it in record time. I found the hospital, University Medical Center, parked my patrol car and went inside. I followed the signs to surgery. There was a lone person at the counter.

"I'm here from Death Valley. I took care of another ranger, Nancy ... did she make it?"

"You're the one who took care of her?"

"Yes," hesitating since I didn't know if she had made it or not.

"She is still in surgery. Wait right here."

I was elated. She was still alive. A door opened and a man in scrubs motioned to me to come in. He took me to a changing room and gave me scrubs, booties and a hair net and mask.

"Go ahead and change out. The surgeon says you can come into the operating room. You can scrub your hands and arms over there."

Wow. I couldn't change fast enough. I had been able to see only a handful of surgeries and they always fascinated me.

I walked into the operating room. The circulating nurse pulled up a stool next to the surgeon's left shoulder and told me to stand on it and not to touch anything.

"So, you're the paramedic from Death Valley who took care of this patient?" the surgeon asked as he worked.

I replied, "Yes." He asked me my name and I said, "Nancy, just like hers," motioning to Nancy, unconscious on the table under general anesthesic.

The doctor held up a kidney-shaped silver pan and reached in with some forceps to pull out a whitish pink piece of tissue that looked like it had been blown up with a firecracker.

"Your patient," he continued, "had a ruptured ectopic pregnancy. She lost almost five liters of blood. You saved her life."

I was stunned. I could only reply, "But she's not big enough to have five liters to lose!"

I watched as they completed the operation and sewed her up. Nancy went to Recovery and I thanked the staff for letting me in. It was now after midnight and I was working on fumes. I hadn't even thought to eat. I changed back out of my scrubs and went outside to my patrol car. I went to the Sahara, a hotel I knew I could park my patrol car with some safety, and registered. I don't even remember my head hitting the pillow.

The next morning I showered, dressed and had a quick breakfast. I went back to the hospital and found Nancy in Recovery. She was sitting up a bit and weak, but had a smile on her face. I told her I didn't know how she could be alive, that she was someone with a will and determination to live beyond anyone's comprehension. I told her I was amazed she never lost consciousness. She told me she remembered them pulling blood from her femoral vein in the emergency room and that it came out pink due to the lack of blood and the presence of saline. I could see she was tired and asked her if I could get or do anything for her. She said she was okay for now, that Joe would be arriving later in the day. We hugged and she thanked me.

When I have a job to do, it gets done. I usually don't lose my cool or get upset or get emotional, so what happened two days later really caught me off guard. I was alone in my trailer, washing my dishes when I burst into tears. I suddenly thought of the medical in all of its detail, remembering every movement, nuance, close call and coincidence. What if I hadn't forgotten to turn my radio off that night, if the pilot had not gotten vertigo, if, if, if? Then, I was okay. But I don't often cry. It was only the second time a medical call has made me cry. This was my friend, someone I knew, a colleague.

Many weeks later in April, when Nancy was back and living at Furnace Creek on light duty, she invited the gals to dinner. Maya and I gladly accepted. As we drove past the Furnace Creek Ranch, with its towering date palm trees and fruit stands, there was a sign that read: Death Valley Dates. With a lurid sense of humor, we got some poor passerby to take a picture of the three of us under the sign as we struck mildly suggestive poses and laughed about it all the way through dinner.

Grand Slam

One of the best things about being a Protection Ranger is the job variety. Most National Park areas are remote and short staffed. As a result, a fully functional Protection Ranger is responsible for just about any emergency that may occur. We are Federal Law Enforcement Officers. We have the training and authority to enforce laws and make arrests as well as serve warrants. Law enforcement (LE) incidents can range from minor (such as shoplifting) to severe, including driving under the influence (DUI) or murder. Visitors to many national parks are surprised to see a handful of the familiar rangers wearing body armor and carrying guns, but rangers are the only police for miles.

For that same reason, most Protection Rangers are also the Structural Fire Department. We receive training and continuing education. Should a fire occur, we pull off our green and gray uniforms, lock our pistols up, and don firefighter pants, boots and jackets. Some of us are entry specialists and some have even more training as engine drivers and operators as well as captains and lieutenants for the fire crew.

By far the most common role Park Rangers occupy is as emergency medical personnel. All Protection Rangers are required to be EMTs and provide basic life support. But a handful go through advanced training and become Parkmedics or paramedics who can provide advanced life support. There are units in the park system that are hours, if not days, away from a doctor or a hospital.

In many parks, rivers, mountains and rough terrain seem to invite hikers and boaters to become lost or imperiled. Many Protection Rangers learn the skills to become technical rescue specialists and are on the Search and Rescue (SAR) Team. Within the SAR Team, individuals may become high angle technical rescuers who rappel off cliffs. There are also swiftwater specialists, mountain climber specialists and helicopter shorthaul specialists. No matter what happens of an urgent or emergent nature, the Park Ranger is the one who will respond and have the skill to solve the problem.

There are times, when the planets align just right, rangers will respond to a law enforcement incident, a fire, an emergency medical incident and a search incident. When this happens in a 24-hour period, it's known as a Grand Slam. Not too often, one ranger will have their own Grand Slam.

In the basin of Death Valley, there are only a handful of roads. Many more lead into the side canyons, hills and mountains that enclose the valley. In March, an abandoned car was found in the desert, totally off of any road. Tracks from the car of a man wound a circuitous route over some hills and toward the Funeral Mountains. The early hasty searchers followed the tracks until they disappeared. Only a baseball cap was found that day. A full-blown escalation was ordered. Helicopters would arrive the next day to provide an aerial advantage for the SAR team members. I was too busy that first day to be a part of the SAR team. My day started much earlier, at 7:00 a.m.

I was returning to the developed area of Stovepipe Wells at 7:40 a.m. when a 1967 Chevrolet sedan pulled out of the parking lot at a high rate of speed and headed west up the Towne's Pass road. I watched as the Chevy fishtailed and crossed the double yellow line twice. As I turned my small Chevrolet S10 truck with a patrol light bar on top to exit the lot, a concessions employee that I knew, Harold, came running up to my vehicle.

"That's Bill," Harold gasped. He quickly told me that Bill was an ex-employee of his who now lived in Panamint Springs, on the other side of the mountains.

"He's drunker than a skunk and is going to kill somebody," he finished.

"You mean because he is driving drunk?" I asked.

"No, he said he's going to Panamint Springs to kill somebody over there!" Harold intoned.

I acknowledged Harold and requested backup, putting the situation over the air. I didn't think my little truck could keep up with the sedan. I asked my Dispatch to alert the Inyo County Sheriff Deputy in Panamint Springs and requested the resident California Highway Patrol (CHP) Officer to respond from Furnace Creek. Within three minutes I caught up with the sedan, which was partly off the side of the road with the driver's door open. I could see Bill, a 28-year-old white male, leaning out of the car, vomiting on the ground. I positioned my truck behind and slightly to the left of Bill's car and about thirty feet back. I heard on the radio that another ranger was only ten minutes away and requested he respond.

Bill stood up when he saw me and started to stagger toward me. I ordered him to stop and return to his car. He said, "Why?" as he continued to walk toward me. I again ordered him to stop, drop what was in his hand and put his hands on the trunk of his car. I never left the "V" of my doorframe. Bill's hand opened and his car keys fell to the ground and he turned around and put his hands on the trunk. He looked over his shoulder and said, "I don't got no gun, just a knife." He then stood up, turned around and walked toward me, placing his right hand in his jeans pocket. I ordered him to take his hand out of his pocket and to stop, but he refused.

I pulled my pistol, pointed it at him and repeated my order. He pulled out a three- to four-inch-long folding knife, stared at it for a moment, then threw it to the ground. He ignored my orders to lie down on the ground and, instead, began to wander and talk to himself. I put out the newest information on the radio and, again, ordered him down. He still refused. When Ranger Ian arrived, he opened the passenger door of my truck, crouched behind it, pulled his pistol and pointed it at Bill. Again, I ordered Bill to lie down, and this time he did. I "covered" him with my pistol as Ian holstered his and placed Bill in handcuffs while he was still on the ground. Ian searched the rest of his person, emptying change, some gaming tokens and his wallet from his pockets. He removed his belt and watch and found no other weapons.

After I holstered my gun, we walked Bill to the passenger side of my truck and had him sit down. Sheriff Deputy Don and CHP Officer Dave arrived almost simultaneously. Bill had red watery eyes, slurred speech and the odor of a digested alcoholic beverage on his breath. Officer Dave stayed while Ian and I completed field sobriety maneuvers on Bill. To do this, we walked him to some level terrain and took off his handcuffs. When we performed a test on Bill's eyes, we were able to see them bounce, a condition called nystagmus, in six different tests.

This test is called horizontal gaze nystagmus (HGN). When a suspect has a six out of six that usually means their blood alcohol level is over 0.1. As Ian put Bill through other maneuvers, I watched and took notes. Most DUI tests are set up to test two different actions by the suspect. We demonstrate them first and then ask the suspect to attempt them. One is simply to balance on one foot and recite the alphabet. A sober person can do this, but an intoxicated person is not good at multitasking. They may hold their foot up and mess up the alphabet. Or they may be concentrating so much on getting the alphabet right, that their foot falls to the ground several times.

Bill performed poorly in all of the tests and I asked him if he would blow into my field alcohol sensor box. He agreed and blew a 0.167. When I told Bill the results, he insisted on blowing a second time. The second time he blew a 0.217! Bill was clearly intoxicated and I placed him under arrest for driving while under the influence of alcohol. After I placed handcuffs back on Bill, I requested a prisoner transport vehicle. It would be very unsafe to take him the almost two-hour drive to the Lone Pine jail in the front of my truck with me. While I waited for the transport vehicle, Bill asked if I could get his cigarettes for him from his car. I told him I would, but he couldn't smoke until he got to jail. When I walked up to the sedan, I observed several open cans of *Budweiser* beer and some spent bottles of beer. Ian received permission to move Bill's car off of the road and secure it.

When the transport vehicle arrived, I placed Bill in a transport belt. This is a thick leather belt with the buckle in the back and handcuffs attached to the belt in front. I then put him in the back with his seat belt on and headed out for the long drive to Lone Pine. Through the entire trip, Bill never shut up. He would get belligerent, then pathetic, then angry. He said his life wasn't worth living anymore. He told me when we got to the jail he would go after me and force me to shoot and kill him. This went on for almost two hours. I mostly didn't say anything to him. I didn't want to encourage him and I have learned from too much experience that you can't reason with a drunk.

When we arrived at the jail, I requested assistance in getting Bill out of my vehicle. He was finally compliant, apparently all talked out. He was given an intoxilizer test and blew 0.16 and 0.14 in succession.

By law, a suspect in custody will receive an arraignment in front of a judge within forty-eight hours of incarceration. When I arrived back in Death Valley, I was told Bill's hearing would be the next day at 4:00 p.m. I knew I could leave Death Valley by 2:00 p.m. and arrive in plenty of time. In addition to being the arresting officer, we often performed as prosecutors. I would arrive to present the case to the U.S. Judge Magistrate who would decide whether to release Bill or hold him over for trial. So I sat in my little office and began typing my report. The jail had the prisoner's copies of his violation notices, but I had the originals. If I did not show up to present the U.S. Government case against Bill, the judge would have the option of throwing the whole case out.

The next morning I went to work on the search at Furnace Creek. My job was easy: sit in the open door of the military helicopter and look down for the missing man. We knew little more than we did the day before. The car registration gave us a name and a background search was completed. There didn't seem to be an obvious reason why this man would wander off in Death Valley in this manner. There were some cigarette butts found on the Beatty cut-off road. They were gathered as evidence, but we didn't know if they were a part of our search scene.

By 2:00 p.m., I had cleared the search, changed to my class A uniform for court, and began the drive out of Stovepipe Wells for Lone Pine. I had only gone one mile when I heard the sound of gunfire. I looked to the south side of the road and there was a man and a woman. The man threw something into the air, pumped a lever-action rifle in his hand and pulled the trigger.

BOOM!!

The rifle's discharge sounded out as a .44 magnum bullet crossed the road! I immediately drove straight toward the pair with my large Bronco and flipped on my light bar and siren. That startled the hell out of them. I stayed in the vehicle with a nice big engine block between the suspects and me, and used the public address (PA) system to order them to stop, drop the gun and put their hands into the air. The rifle went banging to the ground as the 28-year-old man threw his hands up. The woman, a bit younger, also complied. I then ordered them to step forward, away from the rifle, and to lie prone on the ground with their hands out to the sides and their faces away from me. Again, they instantly complied. This was much easier than the day before, I mused.

I got on the radio and asked for backup. I needed the nearest ranger to take this case over so I could get on the road to court in Lone Pine. Ranger Bill had been on foot in the sand dunes and raced to his car. Ranger Dan had been down to help in the search and he, too, headed my way. Now I waited. I never had to draw my weapon because they so readily complied with my commands, I just stayed in the "V" of my open car door. The male suspect began to move and I ordered him to stay still. He froze. Then the female began to move, but when I ordered her to stay still, she continued to bend her arms and kick the ground with her legs. Then the male began to kick and flail. I again ordered them to stop, but their gesticulations became even wilder. Then the male called out, "Ants!"

"What?" I asked.

"Red ants, they are all over us, they're biting hard!" he pleaded.

I had apparently proned them out on an anthill. It was unexpected and unintended but it seemed like a little bit of justice. I allowed them to slowly and individually get up, move to the side and sit with their hands under their buttocks.

Rangers Bill and Dan arrived almost simultaneously. I took only a moment to tell them I couldn't be late for court. They understood and, since I saw the infraction, I signed a violation notice (a ticket) with my probable cause statement and Ranger Bill said he would fill out the rest for me. They chuckled at the red ant story and I waved my thanks as I sped up the road to Towne's Pass. As I approached the Emigrant Junction, I saw a large plume of black smoke on the road ahead. Something was on fire.

I got on the radio to Dispatch and reported a possible fire on the road ahead of me. I would get back to them momentarily. As I came over a rise in the road, a large sedan was completely engulfed in flames. I called it in to Dispatch, requested a fire engine and backup ranger, explaining over the air that I had to get to court in Lone Pine. I went ahead of the inferno and parked my vehicle uphill of the flames. I ran back and pulled two people standing near the vehicle farther away from the fire. I confirmed that they were the only two occupants of the vehicle and that both were unharmed. I asked what happened. They said they were visiting from Minnesota and that the hills were really big out here and that their car began to overheat. I ran down the road and stopped a car coming up. I asked the occupants to back down the road and to put on their hazard lights and try to stop all other cars from coming up. I then ran back up the road and used my vehicle with the light bar on to block traffic coming down the road.

Suddenly there was a horrific explosion as the gas tank blew up in a ball of flames. The vehicle was burning a bit less now, as it ran out of things to burn. My goodness, it went fast. The tires were melted onto the road and a box-like skeleton began to take shape amidst the smoke and flames. Ranger Dan arrived within minutes and we cancelled the fire engine. There was nothing left to save and the fire would soon burn itself out. I turned to Dan, filled him in and pleaded with him to manage the scene. I promised to do the paperwork, a quick sell to any ranger. I jumped into my truck and reported to Dispatch that I was clear, that Ranger Dan was on scene and that I was again headed out to Lone Pine. Before I could even get my vehicle turned around, Chief Ranger Dale called on the radio.

"Negative on Lone Pine, 4R24," (my radio call sign). "Return back to the Stovepipe Wells airport. A man has fallen at the Furnace Creek Inn, hit his head and is having grand mal seizures. We are sending the helicopter for you," Dale replied. So much for Lone Pine.

I raced down the road to the airport and turned in just as the helicopter landed. It stayed hot, that is, the rotors were still turning. I grabbed my advanced life support bag, locked my vehicle and ran crouched to the open door of the aircraft.

"Welcome back," the airman said to me. I gave a wry smile, hopped into a seat and put my seat belt on. It was a thrilling ride, with the doors wide open at well over 100 mph and only 30 feet off the desert floor. We landed on the dirt lot adjacent to the Inn and I made my way to the pool where the victim lay unconscious. He was no longer seizing, so we managed his airway, administered oxygen, started an IV and put him in full spinal precautions. We took him by ambulance to the Furnace Creek Airport and waited for the Flight For Life helicopter out of Las Vegas. The patient began to become more alert as we attended to him, which is always a good sign. After the medical helicopter shut down, we gave a report to the Flight Nurse and turned patient care over to her. We got back in the ambulance to avoid the rotor wash and watched as the helicopter took off and headed southeast to Las Vegas.

I stepped back out of the ambulance and stretched my legs. The sun was bright and it was a nice warm day. Chief Ranger Dale arrived and walked over to me. Before he could say anything, I pleaded with him, telling him how I really did try to get to Lone Pine for court but things kept happening. He smiled, and said we were okay. He called and told the federal magistrate all that had just happened to me: the search, the shooting, the sedan fire and the head injury patient. The judge granted a continuance.

"The judge said he was sure I was telling the truth because no one could make up a story like that," Dale chuckled.

Then I realized I had a Grand Slam. But this one had to be a record, because my Grand Slam happened in only one hour!

Epilogue

In court a few days later, I presented my case. Bill pled guilty to DUI and no contest to having open containers of alcohol in a motor vehicle. He was given credit for time served in jail, placed on three years of probation, and fined $500. He also had to attend a level I Drunken Driver Course and submit at any time to any Peace Officer requesting a blood alcohol test.

The rifle suspect later paid a fine for possession of and discharging a rifle in a park area. The couple from Minnesota's sedan was a total loss, and they were assisted in getting a rental car from Las Vegas. The patient with the head injury eventually made a full recovery without any further seizures. The man who was the focus of the search was never found. He never returned to claim his car, and we speculated whether he had doubled back to the Beatty cut-off road to start a new life or was still somewhere in the Funeral Mountains. Most of us decided this was a man intent on not being found.

The Flag

I have no doubt that it is a dream of many people to live and work in Hawaii. When I had the opportunity to move to Aiea, a suburb of Honolulu, I jumped at the chance. I would be working as a Park Ranger Naturalist/Interpreter at the U.S.S. Arizona Memorial at Pearl Harbor. The Memorial is a spectacular architectural arch that spans, without touching, the sunken remains of the battleship, *U.S.S. Arizona*. On December 7, 1941, the ship was moored with others in Pearl Harbor during the Japanese attack. After a direct hit, it sank in the harbor taking with it 1,177 lives on that ship alone. It has remained in place ever since as a grave for those many young men.

One of the problems with being a seasonal in Hawaii is that you don't make a lot of money and you are there for less than six months, so it's pretty expensive. But the support I received from the local staff was tremendous and welcomed. As it turned out, there were quite a few men named "Mark" who worked there. So they were all called variations of the name to distinguish them. Mark was a co-worker, Maleko was my supervisor, but it was

Marko who met me at the airport in Honolulu with his Volkswagen Beetle in November. I had brought a bicycle and boxes and it was dark and pouring rain outside. I was so grateful for his help. With all of my belongings and the two of us crammed in his bug, I was soon deposited in Aiea in a residential area. One of the permanent rangers, Daniel, rented a two-room apartment and had offered to sublease one of the rooms to me. Daniel welcomed me and helped me to get oriented and established.

I jumped into my duties at the Memorial and became acquainted with the many people who worked there. There were Park Service employees who ran the visitor center on land adjacent to the harbor as well as U.S. Navy personnel who ran the boats that transported visitors to the arched Memorial itself. There were also Pearl Harbor survivors who came almost daily to tell their stories to the fascinated visitors. I never tired of the eyewitness accounts of those brave men.

A typical day began early in the morning as I left my room in Aiea (pronounced "eye-ay-uh") and began the four mile walk downhill to the Memorial visitor center. In the dawn, I could just make out, and often not avoid, the numerous cockroaches that scurried across the sidewalk. I loved those walks. I would listen to music on a little cassette player as the sun came up and the winds shifted with the warming air. Going past the C&H Sugar factory, there was always a smell of molasses in the air and it was fun to look at the towering visage of Aloha Stadium. Once out of the residential area, I would walk along a fence adjacent to the highway leading to the Memorial. The fence acted as a net to collect trash blown into it by the trade winds. I usually wore civilian clothes to and from work, as the humidity would soak my uniform through, and I would always be in danger of losing my ranger flat hat in the wind. It was also nice to be out of uniform and anonymous for the walks, but I still received a lot of stares, as I was a definite minority amongst the native Hawaiian and Asian peoples. I was a *haole*, a non-local.

I learned the Hawaiian language has only twelve letters and an "i" sounds like an "ee." One day, I knew I had been on the island a while when a young man came to the Memorial visitor center with a shirt that had "OHIO" on it. I saw it and immediately pronounced it "oh-hee-oh."

Every morning two of us would go to the grassy lawn in front of the visitor center and place a huge flag on the flagpole. It was warming to see everyone freeze and stand still as we pulled the flag up to the top of the pole and secured it. But Tuesdays were my favorite days and I always volunteered to put the flag up that day. Dressed in my crispest park ranger uniform and flat hat, I and another park ranger would be joined by the Navy band in their white uniforms. They would play the national anthem as we raised the flag. Then, they would continue with a rousing rendition of "Anchors Away." Tuesday mornings were great.

Afterward, we admitted visitors. The line into the visitor center would move quickly as we handed out tickets. These were free, but seating on the Navy boats was limited. We would often give out the last available ticket of the day before noon. We would introduce the movie, walk and answer questions, and take turns patrolling the dirt parking lot to deter any thieves who wanted to work the area. We would also take turns changing into shorts and wading in the rectangular pool of water inside the plaza of the visitor center. It was a magnet for coins and we would scoop them up every day, dry and count them, and send them off to the bank to support Memorial projects. It was amazing the variety of foreign coins that we would find in the fountain.

We also were assigned duty time on the Memorial itself. We would join one of the Navy shuttles and give out information on the Memorial as we moved through the harbor to dock. We would request respect and low voices from the visitors, impressing on them that they were visiting a watery graveyard. Once on the Memorial, we would stay for some time answering questions. One of the most common was about the bubbles of oil that consistently rose to the surface from the ship that created a circular slick on the surface. The *U.S.S. Arizona* had taken on a tremendous amount of fuel prior to the attack and small amounts were still leaking out decades later. There was always someone who asked if it was blood from the deceased.

A flag flew over the Memorial daily. At times, several flags were raised and lowered from this pole in one day to be given to special dignitaries or to commemorate special events. I even purchased one from the gift store and took the time to raise and lower it, replacing it with yet another. I gave that special flag to my parents, Tom and Eileen. My Dad had been in the Infantry in Europe during World War II and my Mom had been a Cadet Corps Nurse. I was proud of both of them and, as I suspected when I gave it to them, they cherished the flag I had flown over the Memorial. I had flown it for them on December 7.

December 7 was a huge day at the Memorial. Politicians, dignitaries, celebrities, survivors, historians and the public all became a part of the organized activity. I had been given an assignment and would work with Ranger Gail. Gail had lived in Hawaii all her life and was one of the most capable and friendliest people I'd ever met. She also was barely five feet tall. But she had a presence much taller than her height and ably helped to organize the proceedings.

On December 7, the grounds of the visitor center would become wall-to-wall people. There were chairs set up on the Memorial for senators, ambassadors, admirals and superintendents who would predominate in the crowd of special guests. I was privileged to be assigned on the Memorial for the duration of the special event. An Honor Guard shot their rifles for the 21-gun salute and two marines played taps, one echoing the stanza the first had just played. It sent chills up my spine. Then huge Navy ships passed by with their entire crew in dress whites, lining the railings in salute as their ship passed the Memorial. There was a drizzling rain throughout all of this but not one participant was deterred. Following several speeches, wreaths and flowers were thrown into the water over the sunken battleship. They lingered, bobbing in the water, then drifted slowly away with the current. Navy shuttles arrived to take the dignitaries away. After a time, I was one of the last on the Memorial. I walked its length and, on the far wall, read the hundreds of names of all of those lost this same day in 1941. Then I raised and lowered a flag for my parents.

At the end of one sunny day at the visitor center, I was assigned the closing procedures. Almost all of the visitors were gone. I was about to close and lock gates and check doors when two Naval Officers came running into the center. They paused to catch their breath as I pondered what emergency brought them here. I was not very good at reading rank insignia, but there was a lot of metal on these two gentlemen.

"Can I help you?" I asked.

"We need to raise and lower this flag over the Memorial," the taller officer replied, holding up a flag folded in typical triangular fashion.

"I think that can be arranged. Come back tomorrow and you can take any of the shuttles over and we will assist you then," I offered.

"No, we have to do it now. A high-ranking officer is retiring tonight and the ball got dropped on getting a Memorial flag for his retirement. We have to do it today!"

"But all of the Navy personnel who run the shuttles are gone. I can't get you over there even if I wanted to," I said.

"We brought our own boat; we just need permission from the Park Service to set foot on the Memorial."

There was great respect for the Memorial, especially among military personnel.

I thought quickly.

"Okay, but I have to go with you."

"No problem," they answered.

I told them I had to finish closing and would join them in a few minutes at the Navy pier, where the shuttle boats were moored. I would go in uniform and change for my walk home afterwards.

I joined them in their motorized skiff and we made our way to the Memorial. I hopped off and tied their lines to the cleat on the wharf. We entered past the brass bell and walked to the far side to see the names. I always have to see the names so I will never forget why the Memorial is there. We then went to the flagpole and they raised then lowered their flag, folding it back into its triangular bundle. It wasn't until after we were back on the boat that the first word was spoken since arriving at the Memorial. It was another very special moment for me. They took me to the Navy pier to drop me off and, again, thanked me profusely. I told them it was my pleasure and turned to leave.

"Hey, if you ever want a tour of our ship while it's in Pearl, we would be glad to arrange a tour," one offered.

I turned back, "I'd love to. Which is your ship?"

They pointed to one that had taken up the skyline for the last two days, the one that had garnished the most awe and attention by everyone who came to the Memorial and could see it so very huge right beside us. It was the aircraft carrier, *U.S.S. Enterprise.*

"You're kidding! The *Enterprise?* You will give me a tour of the *Enterprise?*" I was floored.

"When can you come?"

"Tomorrow is my day off. How about tomorrow?" I asked.

We made arrangements for an afternoon tour and, after changing my clothes, I think I floated home to Aiea.

I arrived at the dock on time and my name was on a list of persons allowed on board. I received permission to board and was greeted by Master Chief Petty Officer Jerry. Jerry was affable and generous with his time. We toured for well over an hour, going from the flight deck to the bridge to the pilot's room and the mess hall. This ship was a floating city! It had a crew of over 5,000 people. There were only a few places Jerry asked me to not take pictures and I readily complied. It was a super tour. One pilot gave me a signed, framed photo of a Russian *Bear,* a long-range reconnaissance aircraft, and decals and patches of the VF114 Flying Aardvarks Squadron. I was overwhelmed and told Jerry so. Jerry said it was nothing compared to the privilege of letting his crew obtain a flag flown over the Memorial. He was right. You can't put a price on the American flag flown over such a special and honored site.

Saturday

As soon as I got on shift at 8:00 a.m., I received a call of a woman who took a vertical fall with unknown injuries at Tuweep Campground. That is on the North Rim about fifty air miles west of the South Rim where I worked. I responded to the helibase with one other member of the Technical Search and Rescue Team, Michael. We outlined three plans depending on what we found to the Operations Ranger at the helibase. We would let them know what we needed when we arrived on scene. Our helicopter was big but not huge, and could only take Michael, me, the Pilot Jerry, and our rescue and medical gear.

We took off at 9:00 a.m. for our thirty-five minute flight. Michael and I had worked together before and we both agreed that a fall at Tuweep was not a good thing. There are some shelves and chutes, but for the most part it's 600 to 700 feet straight down to a sloping plateau of rocks. Michael was an EMT and assisted me on a lot of calls. We only hoped we had something to work with.

We were in the "monsoon season" with high cumulus clouds

that formed during the day, making spectacular thunder and lightening shows, gully washers and flash floods. As we flew west, we saw the clouds begin to form around us and wondered what factor they would play in the rescue.

We finally arrived in the area. Just to the west you could see Vulcan's Throne, a volcanic cinder cone high above the most treacherous rapids in the Colorado River system, Lava Falls. As we neared the sheer cliffs, we began a systematic twenty-minute scan of the shelves, chutes and plateau below the rim. Nothing.

We landed west of the campground. When we left the helicopter, we removed our flight helmets and nomex gloves as the heat of being 2,000 feet lower than our starting point hit us. Not bad, but it would be a scorcher as the day wore on.

A man named Carl greeted us and said the friend of the missing woman was back in the campground. Carl and his wife were camping when this man, Svante from Sweden, said his friend Maria was missing. As Michael and I approached Svante he looked up from his crumpled position on the bare ground and asked if we had found her. I said no. I identified myself as a Federal Officer and asked Svante what happened.

He said that he and Maria had gone to the rim to watch the sunrise at 7:00 a.m. I mused that I recalled the sunrise was at 5:30 a.m. He continued that they were cold in the early morning. He went back to the rental car to get a blanket and to smoke "a last cigarette." His English was excellent so I asked him to elaborate on that statement. He said that this was his day to quit smoking, so he had one last cigarette at the car. He said he was not looking at the rim when, after a few minutes, he heard a rock fall. I asked if he had heard a scream or yelling. He said no. (I once fell seventy-five feet on a granite slab and yelled the whole way down!)

Svante, fearing the worst, ran to the rim to look for Maria but she was nowhere in sight. He ran back and forth but there was no sign of her. He approached two other couples in the small campground and asked for help. One man drove the dirt road for almost an hour-and-a-half to the nearest phone to call for help.

I told Svante I had to ask him some difficult questions. When I asked him about Maria and his relationship with her he said that she was very happy yesterday, but woke up tense this morning. He said her relationship with her parents was strained, and that they had once been engaged to be married, but Maria broke off the engagement a year ago, just wanting to be friends. I asked about the gold wedding band on a chain around his neck. He said it was his engagement band and it had Maria's name inscribed on the inside. I got the feeling that Svante still wanted to be more than just friends. He said they hadn't been intimate for over a year, since the break of their engagement, but continued to travel and do other things together.

I apologized for the following question and asked, "If we find her below the rim, did you push her?"

He looked at me and sincerely said "No," and acknowledged that I had to ask the question.

I asked him if she could have been angry with him for smoking a cigarette on the day he was to quit and walked off in the desert away from the rim. He said maybe. I asked him where he thought she was. He said below the rim. I asked him if I could look in their rental car and he said yes. There was food and there were beer cans in and around the cars. I slipped the key into the trunk and opened it. There were only packs and clothing inside. I obtained both of their passports from Svante. They had been in the United States since August 14. I looked at her passport photo. She was gorgeous.

Christine was one of the other campers in the area. She had been quite helpful in staying with and comforting Svante. She agreed to write and gather witness statements from all who had been in the area this morning. I noticed she was limping and pivoting on one foot. I asked if she had turned an ankle. No, she said, she had cerebral palsy and that was just the way she was. I told her I thought she was remarkable. She just smiled and limped off to continue the task at hand.

I met with Michael who had been talking to Operations and interviewing others. I took photos of the last seen area and we agreed that we needed to go over the edge to see if she was caught in the chimney below the rim. I volunteered and opened the bash pack. It's a Technical Search and Rescue pack for one or two people to get going quickly without all the other big and heavy equipment. There were no real good places to drive an anchor, so Michael took thirty feet of webbing and wound it twice around a boulder that weighed several tons and was wedged near the rim. He secured it with water knots.

I put on my chest and seat harness and placed ascenders, webbing, extra carabiners and prusiks on my belt. A double figure eight knot with a back up clipped me into the webbing anchor. I unclipped my metal figure eight with "ears" and wove the rappel line through it and clipped it back in. I sent it through my chest harness and placed a triple loop prusik on the line as an extra brake. This would be a self-belay. With only one rope, Michael could not safely belay me so I was on my own. I made sure there was a knot on the end of the rope that stuck out of the bottom of the rappel bag in case disaster struck. If I were to rappel all 150 feet of line, at least I would stop (hopefully) 150 feet down and not rappel off the end of the line to continue several hundred feet more, without a rope. I clipped the rappel bag of rope to my belt but Michael suggested I just leave it on the rim and work the tailing line out of the way. Good suggestion. He double-checked all of my riggings, harnesses and equipment.

I then walked to the edge adjacent to the chimney and leaned out. With the security of a rope, I'll do just about anything! I scanned the more than 600 feet below but there was no sign of Maria. After several minutes of this, I made my way to the chute, turned my back to the canyon and took the first two steps.

Those are always the hardest for me. You know the rope will hold, but instinctively, leaning out 45 degrees with a vertical fall of over 600 feet, well, it makes your heart beat a little faster and makes you wonder, albeit briefly, what the hell you are doing this for and why someone else isn't doing it instead!

Then I took the third step. I was instantly calm and in my element and had a purpose and a mission. I pulled the rope back with my right hand to stop it from moving through the metal figure eight to halt my progress. I placed it in front of my thigh to let it run through and assist my descent. I locked it down to ensure I wouldn't slip as I looked around. I ended up about twenty-five or thirty feet into the chute and realized it was not a chimney after all, but a small thirty-foot chute with no Maria inside. I walked to the outside of the chute and peered down. There was no more chute, no more shelf, just a straight vertical wall reaching down to the plateau below.

Not that I needed the reminder that there really was no more reason to go any further, Michael called out from above that I shouldn't go any further. I called to him that I wouldn't. I locked down my rope on the figure eight and began a systematic scan of the plateau. What had been a 45- to 50-degree slope had now appeared as a flat area below. Persons in the past had found it necessary to throw debris off the rim here and I could make out the black rings of tires among the boulders and it gave me a size perspective.

Then I saw a raven. Then another. Scavengers of the desert who have the uncanny ability to know when and where to be after life is gone and only the organic remains. I called this up to Michael and he said to come up.

Back on the top, Michael and a camper named Dan from Monterey were seventy-five feet west of me. Dan was on his belly peering over the rim, holding binoculars in his hand. He was shaking so badly, I thought he was going to drop them. I lay down next to Dan and inched out. Michael asked me very nicely not to go out any further. I still had that fearless attitude I'd developed on the rope. Dan pointed below and I looked. I saw dark, and then I saw red.

With the binoculars, I found Maria. Her dark shorts were torn; her red shirt was pulled up on her torso around her neck. Her head was toward the cliff face and her legs toward the river. She was not moving. She was over 600 feet below me . . . below where she had been.

I looked more closely and saw details that most people should never see. Use your imagination to conjure up what might happen if a human body was to fall that far. What I saw would meet and exceed your thoughts and expectations. She exploded. She was gone, only her remains were present.

I called to Michael who was standing on the rim behind me that I had a confirmed "901." That is radio language for a dead body. This is so it can be said on the air and a person with a radio in line in a cafeteria hopefully has no clue what we are referring to. People on vacation, people not in this business, shouldn't have to hear this.

I went to Svante and told him we found her and she was dead. At first I said she was gone, but I know the mind can play horrible tricks on a grieving person who then decides that someone is only gone … nothing more. I quickly told him that she was dead. He moaned and cried and wailed. I held him as we sat facing each other on the picnic bench seat. I took his two hands in mine and said I would be with him if he wanted to say a prayer for Maria. I closed my eyes, and then opened them as he spoke in Swedish. The only word I recognized was "Maria."

Michael called it in and requested hikers and a counselor for Svante. I set up a safety rope for the spot on the rim where she could be seen and, in less than an hour, guided the helicopter to the spot. There were no landing zones so the helicopter came to the rim. Michael, along with ace hikers, Dave and Chuck, began the long route down. No trail, just good judgment, strong bodies and minds and a job to do.

Tammy also had arrived on the helicopter and went to Svante. I introduced him. She used her experienced counseling techniques in Critical Incident Stress Debriefing (CISD) and I left them alone. Carl came over and offered to drive their rental car back to St. George. This worked well for Tammy's plan. The car was turned over to Carl, and Tammy, Svante and all of their belongings went to the helicopter for the flight back to the South Rim. It was getting hot and Tammy left her Gatorade and her ball cap for me. We worked a lot together and we gave each other a look of not envying the other for the job we each had ahead.

I was left on the Rim with Josh. He came in the second helicopter and was the helispot manager. He set up LZs and accumulated equipment. It was after 2:00 p.m. and I finally felt hungry. I looked through the boxes of rations that came with the second ship. We call them "rat packs." I found a tin of ravioli and ate it cold. I then had my second quart of fluid and felt better.

Chuck, Michael and Dave arrived down on the plateau in thirty-seven minutes. I had set the timer on my watch to keep track of them. By the time I clipped into the safety line and peered over the edge, they had walked past her. It was beyond me how they could have done so, and I got on the radio, turned them around and sent them back toward the body. I then saw their efforts. They were climbing. I forgot how steep the plateau really was. From above, it looks flat. They missed her because she was fourteen feet above the path they had taken.

They spent over an hour with the body, no longer Maria – one of those adaptations rescuers make to keep from thinking about what they really are doing. They took photos, made sketches, and walked the fall line as best they could from the base of the vertical cliff. They gathered the many detached parts and brought them to the main body. They turned it over. They took photos, measurements. They put the remains in a royal blue body bag. It was easily seen from above, blue against the tans and grays and browns of the desert below. Dave called on the radio. They were done. Did we have any soap and water to send down? We found water, but no soap. I didn't like telling them that. When I did, there was silence on the radio.

At 3:30 p.m., the Department of Public Safety (DPS) helicopter out of Kingman, Arizona, arrived. The Park helicopter landed to the west and hooked up a hundred-foot line with a cargo net below.

Jerry is an expert pilot; I'll go anywhere with him. He is truly gifted. He maneuvered the load from the rim to the body recovery team. They unhooked it and he backed off, hovering in wait. The body bag was placed in the net and Jerry moved the helicopter back into position. They hooked it back up and he slowly lifted it higher and higher. I took some photos, then unclipped. I made my way to the campground LZ and Josh to the west LZ. As Jerry approached, I used the hand signals we were taught in helitack school and maneuvered the cargo net to its resting place. Perfect. I made a slicing motion across my forearm and Jerry released the cargo net. He then went to the west LZ where Josh landed him.

A visitor walked over the horizon from the north. I asked one of the DPS officers to keep them away. People on vacation don't need to see this. In the time Josh and I waited on the Rim by ourselves for the team to arrive on the plateau, several groups of visitors came and went. I was in my bright orange flight suit, the one I wear in case we have to shorthaul (hang from below the helicopter for insertion into a rescue site). We gave the same story to each. We were park rangers and we were just ending a practice session for Search and Rescue. Most thought it was marvelous and one man said, "God bless you, I hope you never have to use it." Then I heard his wife admonish him not to get too close to the edge.

I walked to the royal blue body bag and put on latex gloves. There were body fluids on the outside of the bag and we needed to protect ourselves. There was the smell of ruptured bowel. Not unexpected, but an instant reminder that this was not the first time I had done this. This smell was all too familiar.

A plastic tarp was placed around the bag and it was then placed on a stretcher. Josh, two of the DPS officers, and I lifted it and placed it in the helicopter. Humor saves those who deal with such things, and those who don't understand would think it highly irreverent, the remarks that were made soon after. Sanity remarks, that's all. Jerry came over and pilots talked pilot things and EMS folks talked EMS things and then, they left. It was 4:00 p.m.

Chuck called up from below. He said they were starting up and would have their radios off. They said they would do their own CISD on the hike out.

The fire reconnaissance helicopter came and took a lot of equipment. I repackaged the bash pack, repacking it later that evening on my return to the South Rim. Josh was to stay until the hikers made it to the rim. Jerry and I loaded the helicopter. In my pocket was a sheet of paper: the campground sign-in sheet. Maria had made an entry the day before. She wrote she was in a party of two, they were camping, and they were from Sweden. Then there were two long words in Swedish I didn't understand. I photographed the page and removed it from the book, later giving it to the Park Criminal Investigator. I still wonder what she had written.

Jerry and I took off for the South Rim. The hikers and Josh followed soon after in the other helicopter. We spoke briefly about what we had done that day: the sadness, terror, and tragedy. Then we were done. The clouds that had sprinkled on us off and on through the afternoon were parting and the distant lightening was gone. We saw wild horses below us on the Kaibab Plateau. I was exhausted, physically and mentally tired. I made it home safely.

Saturday Sequel

■ Grand Canyon, Arizona

Everyone has heard of rigor mortis, the rigid tightening of the body's muscles after death. It is often used to estimate the time of death. What is less known in the lay world but seen often in the medical world is livor mortis. Livor means black and blue and describes the eventual pooling of blood by gravity in a body that is no longer circulating blood. We see it often, and when we come on scene to a "man down" call who appears dead, we know with the beginning of lividity, there is no sense in starting CPR as the blood hasn't been circulating for a long time. The body, should it be on its back, is a pasty pale color on top. But from the sides to the back is the purple mottling of lividity that says this person is and has been dead for a while.

When the DPS helicopter headed off to Kingman, Arizona, with the dead body of Maria from the Tuweep cliffs, I flew back to the South Rim and the body recovery crew hiked up for the next flight. Later that night, a few of us went to a CISD meeting, meant to be a stress reliever. For me it was more stressful to attend, having put in such a long day and then return to a private meeting where you are given the opportunity to release your thoughts. After so long in this business, I have learned to deal with these morbid situations and then move on. The CISD was not necessary for me, but I went to support others.

Afterwards, I talked to Michael, and he said some things that set the hairs on the back of my neck on edge. I immediately began to think of explanations, but in the many weeks since that day, the truth of what he saw has finally convinced me that what we dealt with that day was not so clear-cut.

Michael said he was surprised that there was so little blood on the scene of the fall landing site. My answer was that if she hit further up the blood would be further up and not at her final resting place. He said they had followed the fall line, and still found very little blood. And there was plenty of opportunity for it to have exited the body.

More chilling though was Michael's observation of the lividity. A few days later he showed me the photos he had taken on scene of the body. He was an experienced EMT and didn't want to speak "out of school," but what he was taught and had observed over the years made what he saw that day seem very, very wrong. Yes, Maria had textbook signs of lividity. The blood had indeed pooled to the backside of her body. The only problem was, she landed face down.

You would think that the front of her body, the one face down on the ground with the pull of gravity would be where the lividity would be. Instead, it was the backside up that was livid. Could it be sunburn? One look at the photos proved that theory wrong. As much as we didn't want to face it, it appeared that Maria was already dead, and had been dead for some time when she dropped those many hundred feet over the cliffs. After death, clotted blood that has congealed over time does not leak out; neither does lividity defy gravity and pool to the top. Could she have landed on her back and after a few hours somehow been turned over prior to our arrival?

Perhaps, by an animal, but there were no signs of animals disturbing the body. We had it in sight virtually the entire time from discovery to recovery and it had not been disturbed.

We examined the campground sign-in sheet and compared notes. What Svante told Michael was not what he had told me. This was not their first visit to Tuweep. They had been there two days previously. Svante had signed in. On the same page a man from Germany had written in English, "nice place to kill your wife." Pretty black humor, humor seen by Svante. Then there was the entry the night before the body was found. Maria had written it in Swedish. I e-mailed Greg, a life-long friend whose wife was Danish. My transcription was flawed but the early interpretation by Janne was, "I'm frightened." Geez! Could our worst fears be a reality? Later, after sending them a photocopy of the sheet, a more literal translation was "frighteningly beautiful." Still it was a strange adjective choice on Maria's part.

Then we learned that the "fall" had occurred much earlier than reported. When Svante discovered Maria was gone, he did not immediately call the other campers for help. He drove the thirty minutes to the closed Ranger Station for help, and then back. He then alerted other campers. But the most incredible part of the interviews Michael and Tammy had with Svante versus mine, is Svante revealed that the reason they were not engaged anymore was that Maria had had an affair in January and called it off with Svante. It's not hard to think that he was a scorned lover who decided that if he could not have her then no one could. Did he kill her that night in the campground and lay her on her back in the car for hours with blood clotting and pooling onto her backside? Did he then, the next morning, drop her cold body over the cliff and by fate have her land face down to reveal the lividity typical of a face up death?

This would all be proven by the Medical Examiner: "Quincy" to the rescue. Welcome to reality. The South Rim is in Coconino County, which has Flagstaff, a booming progressive town with an experienced Medical Examiner (ME). Tuweep is in little populated Mohave County. They do not have an ME. They contract out to various physicians, none of which are forensic pathologists, who look at the body and say, "Yep, they're dead," and sign the death certificate. And this is what happened here. Before anything else could be done, Maria was on her way back to Sweden, taking with her the clues to her death.

The Criminal Investigators (CIs) in Grand Canyon were not convinced that this was an accident after Michael and I presented our observations and evidence. Bev, one of the CIs, began a writing campaign with the State Department. She prepared a series of questions for a Diplomatic Liaison in Sweden and the Swedish Police to ask of Svante, Maria's family, and friends. While the evidence was circumstantial, I had gone from 80% sure it was an accident to 80% sure it was not.

One day Bev called me in with some new information. The questions would be asked, interviews would be made, but even if Svante confessed, nothing would be done. Shocked, I asked her why. Bev said that laws in Sweden were very different from those in the U.S. There, violent crimes are few and the penalties weak. Also, burden of proof and how the law applies in Sweden are different. In the U.S., for instance, if two persons enter a home to burglarize it and one man kills a resident during the commission of the crime, the partner who did not pull the trigger can also be found guilty of murder and be sentenced to death or life in prison. In the same scenario in Sweden, unless they can prove which one did the killing, both will go free on that charge as Swedish law states only the person who actually pulled the trigger is culpable. And the penalty in Sweden for first-degree murder is a maximum of twelve years in prison!

Then Bev gave me the final bit of Swedish trivia. They do not believe in the death penalty and will not extradite any Swedish citizen to a country that has the death penalty. So even if Maria was murdered and Svante admitted it, he would never be returned to this country for trial.

So we look back and realize that, yes, it could have been an accident and Maria could have fallen to her death as Svante described. But I don't think so.

P Street

The pagers sounded at 3:23 a.m. I had not been asleep long as I had worked the night shift until 2:00 a.m. The announcement over the pager was for a house fire in Trailer Village. I quickly pulled on some sweat pants and a top and literally slapped my contact lenses into place. Kent, my husband and the Structural Fire Chief, got on the phone to Dispatch and ordered a General Alarm. The dispatcher had only paged out the Structural Fire Group and Kent wanted the world. We heard the fire siren and the all-group pagers sound.

It was one of the first really cold nights of that winter. Sub-freezing temperatures and no moon made running out of the house, down the porch wall to the ground and over to Kent's truck a bit eerie. It was cold and dark. Kent drove the quarter mile to the Fire Station where several people had congregated ahead of us. Kent dropped me off and threw on his turnouts and headed for the scene. I saw that there was an engineer, Paul, and a captain, Pat, already on board Engine 1. I would be a fire-fighter this call. It's fun to be the engineer, and incredibly taxing to be the captain, both roles I have done in the past, but the *real fun* is in the firefighting, getting down and dirty and feeling the accomplishment of putting down some flames. It tells you a lot about a firefighter when they look forward to going into a place filled with heat and flames while everyone else is running out.

I threw my turnouts into the back of the engine in the enclosed compartment and asked for the red light. Our interior lights in the engine have two switches, red and white. With red, you can see enough to finish dressing without ruining your night vision. I pulled on my bunker pants, threw my suspenders over my shoulders and plunked down in a seat next to Tom, throwing my seat belt on. We accelerated out of the station with lights and sirens to P Street, Trailer Village. There were five of us on the engine.

In the past eight years as a firefighter at Grand Canyon, I have answered lots of fire calls. I usually would wear the fireproof personal protection equipment (we call PPE) made of nomex. Two days before this call we were issued brand new PPE made of a material called PBI. It was thicker, more insulated and very stiff. They had only been worn once for five minutes when I had first tried them on. Afterwards, I hung my jacket, helmet and hood above a bench under my nameplate. On the bench I placed my pants. I had pulled them down to the boot tops so I could step into them easily and had placed the suspenders between the boots. We also refer to the PPE as bunkers and turnouts. I had a heck of a time putting on my jacket and securing everything while going code 3 to the fire. They weren't as familiar as my old turnouts and their newness made me feel a bit like the *Michelin* man.

I placed my portable radio in my bunker top pocket and put

on the internal intercom headset. Pat said we would grab a hydrant and advance to the fire. The report came in that it was a fully involved trailer with flames going twelve to fifteen feet into the air. There were two occupants who got out alive, but were burned and suffering from smoke inhalation. I wondered if I would be pulled to be Paramedic/RN for the injured occupants. Two ambulances, Medic 1 and Medic 2, and Engine 1, Engine 2 and Rescue 4 responded with medics and more firefighters and we ended up with twenty-three persons on the fireground. There were plenty to handle the medical emergencies. I was saved and could still work the fire.

As I pulled on my self-contained breathing apparatus (SCBA) I listened to Pat's plan. He was the River District Ranger and not as familiar with Trailer Village as I was. I told him where the hydrant was so he didn't have to look it up in our map book and offered to "catch" the hydrant for a forward lay. He said, "Good."

In my mind I prepared for my task. The engine would stop with the tail end adjacent to the hydrant. When given the okay, I would exit, go to the rear of the engine and pull down the five-inch hose with the Storz connector. I'd pull quite a bit of hose, grab the hydrant wrench and wrap the hose around the hydrant. I'd cross the end over and hold it in place with my boot and signal the engineer. He'd drive toward the fireground as length after length of huge five-inch hose was pulled off the bed of the truck. I'd let the hydrant take the tension of the pulling truck as the hose fell away. I couldn't possibly stand there and hold it myself. When the tension was released from the falling line, I'd unwrap the hose, unscrew the connection on the hydrant, and twist the hose onto the hydrant. At the other end, the engineer would engage the pump, having chocked the engine in place, and go to the rear of the vehicle, disconnecting the other end of the five-inch hose from the bed. He'd take it to his pump intake, open the valve, and swing his hand in an arc over his head signaling he was ready for water.

I'd place the hydrant wrench on the top and open it all the way. It is a screw valve and I would have to open it completely to get all available water. The pressure of the water out of the hydrant can be anywhere from 40 psi or less to more than 100 psi (pounds per square inch). Usually it's 60 to 80. That is not enough to push water through hundreds of feet of hose, allowing a discharge of at least 150 gallons per minute (gpm) out of each hose. That is where the fire engine or "pumper" comes in. It takes the water from the hydrant and pumps it up to a higher pressure and out through the various hoses or lines the firefighters are using to put out the fire. If the pressure and water flow from a hydrant are low, we may have to catch several hydrants and hook them to the engine.

As it turned out, my review of hydrant catching was all for naught. Kent was on scene and assumed Command and Operations. He ordered us to bypass the hydrant and go directly to the fire. He ordered Engine 2 to catch the hydrant and pump water to Engine 1. That way we could immediately start our attack with the 1,000 gallons we keep on board the engine. At 150 gpm, that gives us only six to seven minutes of water. That was all the time the crew of Engine 2 had to catch the hydrant, connect and get water to their engine, then extend hose to Engine 1's pump to refill the tank and give us an "infinite" supply of water. Engine 2's crew ended up laying seven hundred feet of five-inch hose from the hydrant to the engine.

As we pulled onto P Street, we could see the flames from one hundred yards away. In the dark night they flashed and reflected brightly on the other trailers and homes in the area. They were even brighter than the light bar on the patrol vehicle parked down the road. The pinyon pines above the trailer were also on fire and burning brightly. Pat gave us our assignments and we exited as Paul stopped the engine and blew the air horn once and long. Attached to my seat was my SCBA. I had pulled the forty-pound tank and apparatus onto my back while still seated and turned on my air, checking my regulator for the 2,500 psi that the tank contained. As I left the engine, I had my mask in my hand and I immediately leaned over to pull the SCBA higher onto my back. The turnout coat cushioned me from the metal frame as I pulled on the side straps to hike it up. Then I tightened the waist belt and pulled off my helmet.

Before I put my turnout coat on I had pulled on my nomex hood. It is tan-colored and fire resistant and covers my hair, head, neck, ears and chin. Only my mouth, nose and eyes were exposed. I pulled the hood off to the back of my neck and slipped on the facemask. The rubber seal fit perfectly against my face and I looked through a clear shield with a hole in the mask opposite my mouth. This is not a job for claustrophobes. I pulled the mask webbing over my head then pulled the nomex hood back on, again covering everything, including the mask webbing. I then attached the regulator to the hole in my mask, twisted it into place and, with my first inward breath, the air flowed. (A positive pressure is maintained in the mask and it will do so until I push a special button on the mask). I put on my helmet, turned the screw in the back to tighten it down, and secured and tightened the chin strap. I made sure the collar was up and the neck strap was in place on my bunkers. I pulled on my gloves. In training exercises, we must put the tank, mask, helmet and gloves on in under a minute. With the adrenaline in my system, I accomplished that easily. We did buddy checks, made sure everyone was set to go, and proceeded. This occurred all in a matter of two to three minutes.

I was given the lead on the initial attack crew. Cody and Tom pulled the front transverse line off the engine. It's one-and-three-quarter inches in diameter and two hundred feet long. With 170 psi from the pump we had a guaranteed 150 gpm from the automatic nozzle on the end. We can straight stream the water or get a nice fog spray. The engineer has to be exact in his calculations. Too little psi to the nozzle and you don't get the gpm you need to put out the fire and to protect the firefighter. Too much and the line is unmanageable. They used to joke that all an engineer had to do was crank the pump up so high that the firefighters at the end of the hose were lifted up off the ground and just lower the psi until their feet touch and you're all set. In reality, calculations involve hose diameters, lengths of hose, resistance coefficients, nozzle pressure, and elevation the hose is above or below the pump. All are taken into account to get the water to the fire. As an engineer with multiple lines out, I have worked whole fires and never looked up from my pump panel! Kent says being an engineer can keep you busier than a one-legged man in an ass-kicking contest.

We advanced the line to the south side of the trailer. The trailer was about forty feet long and a third of the roof had collapsed. We normally would have entered through an uninvolved area and put the fire out from that end so that we wouldn't blow the fire into an uninvolved area. But in this case, Kent did not want to risk firefighters in an already collapsing, unoccupied structure – pretty much a lost cause. So we attacked from the outside. I directed Cody, who had the nozzle, and Tom, who was manipulating the hose, to the area of attack at the base of the fire.

He hit it and immediately steam came up. The flames put up a good fight but we were easily and quickly suppressing it. Then the call came out from the engineer over the radio, "Three lights left," and then, "Two lights left." The lights are a measure of the amount of water left in the tank of the fire engine. We started with four lights. Engine 1 did not have a permanent supply yet so we were getting a heads up on how much we had to work with. I told Cody to use just enough to stay even. In a short time it was a moot point. The call came in to us that they had hydrant water and we opened back up and the flames went down. Flames are much prettier than the steam and smoke, but that's okay. The steam was a wonderful sign of accomplishment. Then, I saw it.

Not three feet from the flames was a one hundred-gallon propane tank. Youzer! And next to that was the utility connection with the extension cords still plugged in. I called it in and we immediately began hitting the propane tank to cool it down. We have a word for what happens when propane tanks get too hot ... BLEVE: a boiling, liquid, expanding, vapor, explosion. Another word is *sayonara*. If that baby went, you would have to look far and wide for enough pieces to make one firefighter, let alone the three of us standing there. Once we had a working fire with a propane tank involved adjacent to a burning trailer, but in that case the propane had ignited and flames shot over one hundred feet into the night sky! (In one spectacular fire in another state, a railroad tanker of propane bleved and the tank car was found over a mile away!)

The electric company man, Don, came over and we got close

enough to assist him in turning off the electricity. I then told the crew to cover me as I walked slowly toward the propane tank. It's stupid really, walking fast or slow. At that distance it really doesn't matter. I pulled my glove off to feel the tank with the back of my bare hand. It was warm, not hot. Thank goodness. I uncapped the tank and turned it off before its hose to the house ruptured and ignited the propane.

By this time, the fire was mostly out. Kent judiciously allowed an entry team of four, headed by Chris, to enter the trailer opposite our location. We no longer needed to put water on the fire and were just on standby. We saw flames inside and I reminded my crew to stay down with the nozzle closed. If we'd hit the fire then, all we would be doing was pour super heated steam onto the firefighters inside. Not a good thing. I heard an alarm as Cody's SCBA got low. Tom moved up to nozzle, Cody left and Fred was assigned to my team on the hose. Then Tom's alarm sounded and Fred bumped up to the nozzle as Tom left and Dave came from the staging area to take the hose. I looked down and saw I still had half a tank. Even while SCUBA diving I'd always been able to make a tank last a long time.

The fire was out. Franco, the Criminal Investigator, arrived from the Clinic where he had interviewed the injured occupants. He and Kent investigated the fire scene. I went in with a mop-up crew to check for hot spots. It was black inside. The tub was full of water (ours), the TV screen was cracked and the couch was only springs. Incredibly, a poster on the wall in the back was only blackened with soot. I opened a cabinet in the back and declared to my fellow firefighters that the *Playboy* collection had been saved. I thought we were going to tilt the trailer over as the three guys rushed back for a peek.

We exited and were just starting to clean up and assign a fire watch when a call came in for a 78-year-old woman in distress. Kent pointed to me and off I went. Others helped me pull off my SCBA and I jogged in blackened turnouts to the ambulance. I jumped in and was off. I smiled at the spectacle I was about to present to this woman and her family. I smelled of smoke, was covered in soot and ice, and walked like John Wayne in my new bunkers. Oh well, never a dull moment. Off to the medical ... but that's another story.

Epilogue

The next day, Kent relayed to me the results of the investigation. The owner of the trailer on P Street, Bob, and his roommate, Jim, had made french fries earlier in the evening and left the pan of hot oil on the stove. They then had six to nine beers each. Bob fell asleep in the recliner and Jim on the couch. At 3:20 a.m., Bob started to choke and cough which, luckily, awakened him slightly from his sleep. Then the smoke alarm went off and awakened him fully. He looked over and the pan of oil was on fire. He tried to shake and awaken Jim, but he was drunk, had carbon monoxide poisoning and was not easily aroused. Finally, Bob got Jim up and out of the trailer and returned to the fire. Bob grabbed the pan of burning oil and tried to throw it out the door. He hit the doorjamb and spread burning oil all over the front of the trailer and over his hands, suffering first and second degree burns. We later learned he had a fire extinguisher under the sink adjacent to the burning stove under piles of junk.

Bob then ran out of the trailer, reached back in and grabbed the phone. He pulled it as far as he could to just outside the trailer and called 911. He was still coughing and intoxicated so all the dispatcher heard through slurred words was a "fight" at P Street. When the dispatcher asked how many persons were involved, Bob said two, thinking she was asking about the occupants of the trailer. When Dispatch asked if there were any weapons involved, Bob got the clue that he hadn't communicated well and tried again. When Dispatch realized there was a fire, the tone-outs began.

Snowbound

The first big snow of the El Niño winter hit the Grand Canyon just before Christmas. Here, at 7,000 feet, we received only eight inches of snow. Surprisingly, east of Desert View at 5,800 feet received up to three feet of snow in places and drifts over five feet!

Unfortunately for Desert View Ranger John, his two horses were out there. John had never really had much exposure to horses in his life. When he came to the South Rim and learned how to ride he became one of the Horse Patrol Rangers. In fact, he loved it so much that when he transferred to Desert View, thirty miles east of the South Rim, he bought a horse named Sly. Sly was a pretty palomino, not very tall, and was housed on a private ranch east of the Desert View Ranger Station. At the time there was another ranger, Lem, who also had a horse. Lem introduced John to the care, feeding and daily maintenance routine. After Lem left, John acquired a second horse in the summer, a rich brown quarter horse named River.

When John first got River he asked if I'd come out and take a look at him, give him his vaccinations, and check on a laceration on his chin. I had worked as an assistant in California for a veterinary surgeon. His practice emphasized primarily large animals, horses, cows, sheep and pigs, but we dabbled in small animal medicine too. I had obtained my certificate as an Animal Health Technician and welcomed the opportunity to use those skills.

When I joined John in Desert View to see River for the first time, we rode out in his truck to the ranch. We took the main highway southeast for about twelve miles then turned west onto a horrendous dirt road for another three miles to the ranch. The few buildings were old and tattered, but functional. The sides and roofs of some of the buildings had sheet metal but the old wood still dominated. The corral area fencing was less than fancy. Juniper limbs and branches were the posts and barbed wire bound them together. Inside was a shed that housed the hay and grain and dust of many years. It was very dark inside, sealed to try to keep rodents out. There was no electricity so a flashlight was a necessity. Adjacent was a nice overhang that housed a food trough and gave the geldings (male horses who have been neutered) some shade and windbreak.

We gave the horses some grain and I examined River. As I stood next to him, I estimated he was about fourteen hands high at the shoulder (about four inches to a hand). He was stocky and long ago had been emasculated. This is done to decrease the testosterone in a male's system so he's not as proud and feisty and is a gentler ride.

It's a quick step from stallion to gelding. When I assisted the veterinarian, we gave the horse a fast-acting sedative. By placing a thumb on the jugular vein at the neck, a vessel the size of a garden hose stood out. A quick injection and the horse would begin to stumble and then collapse on his side within a minute. My express job on those calls was to catch the horse's head so it wouldn't slam into the ground when the horse went down. It was quite a sight some times. Some horses stood and quivered and melted to the ground, allowing me to cradle the forty- to fifty-pound skull. Others fought the anesthesic and would begin to walk, stumble and pull back and to the side. I would hold the reins, not wanting to get too close in case a surge of energy would bring the steed barreling into me. I would dance around, in and out, side to side like a boxer in a ring. Then, when it looked like he was going down, I would make my move and step in to cushion the blow to the falling head. It was more like trying to catch fine china during an earthquake.

Then we would work quickly. I would hand the vet the emasculators. He would slip them on above the scrotum and close them, cutting off the circulation to the testicles and severing the spermatic cords. The scrotum would then be sliced open and the pearly white testicles removed. These were often thrown across the horse and over its head onto the ground. Resident dogs would then scurry to gobble them up. If you did not throw them over the head of the horse, there were enough superstitious folks around who would decide then and there that this vet had no clue about horses and he wouldn't be called back. You see, everybody knows that if you didn't throw the testicles over the head of the horse he would stay proud and become unmanageable. This little gesture often sealed in some people's minds whether you knew what you were doing or not.

The scrotum would then be trimmed away from below the emasculators and the sutures applied. The emasculators would be removed and that was that. The horse would get up in a matter of minutes and stagger away wondering what had happened. There were times when the sedative wore off so quickly that a horse would struggle up and we would be following it around to finish the job!

At the ranch, I examined River, running my hand down his legs, feeling for symmetry, bone spurs, swelling and the extra warmth that comes with inflammation. He seemed sound on all fours. His laceration was healing nicely so we irrigated it with povidone iodine and let it be. We decided to add penicillin shots just in case. I showed John how to roll the refrigerated vial between his hands to warm it up. Then, placing a needle on the syringe, I pulled the plunger back to admit air. This would be injected into the vial. The air would replace the fluid I would draw out and balance the pressure in the sealed glass container. After drawing up the medication, I removed the needle from the syringe and held it like a dart between my thumb and index finger. I walked to River and stood on his right side at his rump. While holding the needle, I slapped his rump three times quickly with the back of my hand. When I brought my hand down for the fourth time, I turned it around and jabbed the needle deeply into the muscle. River never knew what happened. He thought it was just a fourth slap. I then attached the syringe, pulled back to be sure it wasn't in a blood vessel, and slowly injected the vaccination. Then I withdrew the entire syringe/needle combination. John repeated the procedure on the left rump, this time injecting the antibiotic. He did fine for a first time. Many people are too timid when they give horses their shots and that is when a horse seems to know something is up.

Since that day in August, an addition to John's stable of geldings was Fox, a large palomino that belonged to Lori, a fee collector at Desert View. Now, on this cold December day, all three were snowbound. There was no access up the dirt road with the snowdrifts. John put the word out for help. On Christmas Eve he skied in to feed them. On Christmas Day some folks snowshoed in to celebrate the day. The day after Christmas, yesterday, two others skied in. John was running out of people to help. He was the only ranger on at Desert View and could not go during the day to take care of them. He called and asked if I would help. There was no one else to go with me so I agreed to solo cross-country ski into the ranch. From the highway, cutting across the prairie, it was only a mile. I just had to get up early enough to drive to Desert View, ski in, feed the horses, ski out and drive home in time to go to work at 5:00 p.m.

I awoke at 9:45 in the morning after getting off work at 2:00 a.m. I had a bowl of hot oatmeal to get myself going. The other night it was 0 degrees Fahrenheit. Last night it was a toasty 9 degrees and currently it was 22 degrees in the sun. I packed my fanny pack with two bottles of water, snacks, camera, radio and survival necessities. I had my off duty weapon in a fanny pack I would wear in front. I layered up. Silk inner top, long-sleeved shirt, fleece outer jacket and pullover anorak as needed. I had my cross-country ski boots on, snow pants over inner pants and gaiters from my knee to my boots. I was ready to go. I was on my second trip to load skis and necessities into the car when I heard a sound in the distance. Instantly, I knew what it was ... the general alarm for a structure fire. It was 10:11 in the morning. I looked at my layers and dreaded the thought of ripping most of them off to jump into my structural fire turnouts. My pager went off as I placed my contact lenses in my eyes ... fire at Coconino Apartments 2006, smoke and flames from the oven. Sigh.

I jumped into my patrol car and arrived at the engine bay. Paul was already there and so he would be engineer. There were at least four other firefighters so I grabbed my turnouts, threw them into the ambulance (which goes on all fire calls) and jumped in with Mike. Off we raced with lights and sirens, being oh so careful over the icy patches on the road. At the fire scene I saw there were enough firefighters for the entry team so threw on my turnout coat and helped a new ranger, Phil, to catch the hydrant. I unloaded the fan from the engine then went over to Donnie, who was taking a report from the resident of the apartment. Just then the call came from Kent, the Fire Chief, that the fire was out. They had entered with a charged line from the engine, but were able to extinguish the fire with a large carbon dioxide extinguisher carried on the engine. This really cut down on water damage. They set up the fan to blow the smoke from the apartment.

Donnie told me that the resident, Amy, had put a plastic dish drainer on the bottom of the oven a day or two before as a place to store it. She had forgotten it today when she turned her oven on to cook and was soon greeted with noxious black smoke and flames of plastic on fire. She'd have to use a really heavy duty cleaner on her oven to get that mess out. While helping to clean up the fire engine, I got some not so very clever comments on my attire from Donnie. I would guess that I was the only one on the fireground wearing cross country ski boots and gaiters.

I was soon cleared from the fire scene and dashed back to my residence after putting Medic 1 back at Station 1. I pulled out of my driveway and made good time to Desert View in about forty minutes. I met John who briefed me on who got what feed and followed him east out of the Park about ten miles. He had to return to Desert View and be available for calls, but wanted to show me the access area.

It was a picture postcard. The snow glistened and sparkled. An occasional juniper tree and pinyon pine dotted the landscape. There were rolling hills made pure and white with the abundant snow. I could see the ranch buildings far off in the distance, just over a mile away. I placed a non-stick fluid on the bottom of my waxless skis, pulled on my new polar fleece hood that my husband Kent gave me for Christmas, snapped on my two packs, pulled on my gloves and reached in for my ski poles. They weren't there. They were at home, leaning against a bookcase where I placed them this morning. I was about to put them in the car when the general alarm sounded and totally forgot to load them afterwards. John offered to drive to his house and get his poles, but that would take thirty minutes and I was already delayed by the fire call. It didn't look too tough. I decided to try cross-country skiing across the rolling prairie land without poles. I had never skied without poles before, but I *Nordic Track* exercise everyday without them, so what the heck. I slapped on my skis and pointed down the slope at an angle. No problem. I schussed about thirty feet, made a not so graceful kick turn and pointed the rest of the way down. At the bottom I fell flat on my face. The snow was three feet there and, as I put my hand down to push myself up, I fell to my armpit in the snow. I looked back up at John and couldn't tell if he was looking at me with pity or was just trying very hard not to laugh.

Undaunted, I centered my weight over my skis, turned and started off toward the ranch. There were a few moments of "almost" as my center of gravity left me, but that first fall was the only fall I suffered on the entire trek. I got into a rhythm, swinging my arms in an arc with the strides of my legs and skis. It was quiet and peaceful. Small sparrows, called juncos, flitted from the exposed branches of sagebrush that stuck out through the snow. There were rabbit and rodent tracks across the snow, ending in depressions that led down below bushes. I went through a few fenced areas and, in less than twenty minutes, arrived at the ranch. I took off my skis and lifted the wires that held the two gates closed. Waiting for me, and not very patiently I might add, were River and Sly. Fox was in a paddock separated from these two hooligans. All three had thick winter hair, almost like fur covering their bodies. As I entered, River came right up to me and shoved his face in my chest as if to say, "I'm saved!" I gave him hugs and scritches. Sly was more aloof but no less insistent. He pawed the ground in impatience. I took the time to take some photos then began the task at hand. With the pitchfork, I carried sections of hay bales to different containers to minimize the competition for the food. I followed with some grain. I could see the hero worship in their eyes. They abandoned the hay for the grain and were in heaven.

With the other end of the pitchfork, I broke up the ice that had formed on the surface of their water trough and removed some of the chunks. I then carried water to Fox's trough, which was solid ice. All my tasks done, I bade good-bye to the "boys" and headed back. I was warm from the exertion and pulled my hood down. The cold air felt good as I effortlessly glided back over my tracks. I was proud of my balance and felt a sense of accomplishment of having made the trek without poles. I arrived at my vehicle after struggling up the steep slope to the highway and looked back toward the ranch. I had a blast. I suppose snowbound is a relative term.

Forty-One Hours

■ Grand Canyon, Arizona

Different seasons of the years in national parks often empha-
size different types of calls or quantity of calls. In Grand
Canyon, our summer season surely is our busiest time for
search and rescue calls, general service calls and medical calls
because of the volume of visitors. In the early 1990s, we exceeded four million visitors for the first time. Just five years later, we
approached five million! This increase in visitation is staggering,
especially when you take into account that there are just over
fifty commissioned rangers in the Park, and less than twenty of
those handle most of the calls. A ranger must switch "hats" quickly, depending on the call. We all have different levels of expertise,
but it's daunting to realize that no matter what happens, we must
be prepared to handle it. We are the police, the fire department,
the emergency medical services, the search and rescue specialists,
the resource managers, the naturalist/interpreters, the wildland
firefighters and more.

In addition, as the seasons change, so does our emphasis. For
me, the summer dayshift on the South Rim is full of variety ...

service calls, medicals, search and rescue, law enforcement. Then in the fall, I go to night shifts for six months. As the days get shorter and the nights longer and colder, the visitation changes and decreases. We see a lot of older people in the fall. "Snow Birds" who come after the summer crunch when many of the kids are back in school. They bring with them their time-grown medical problems. While we may get a cardiac patient any time of the year, I call the fall the "cardiac season." Chances are they will have their cardiac event on the third floor of the El Tovar Hotel where there is no elevator, and after midnight when there are only two rangers on duty. Add to that, the patient may be large in stature and a challenge to bring down those three flights of stairs.

In the fall we see an increase in alcohol use. It's too cold outside to recreate, so many stay inside and some drink too much. Add cabin fever, the holidays and isolation, and the number of calls involving domestic violence, assault, and public intoxication increase. Depression and despondency rise and suicide attempts increase. We see drunk drivers try to negotiate dry and icy roads, foreign visitors who don't know the rules of the land, and many who don't realize the speed limits are posted to give drivers adequate reaction time on the road to keep from hitting an elk, deer or coyote. We have a number of autos versus wildlife calls and everyone loses.

There are times though, when calls come that are not only unexpected but also not associated with a National Park. They come with a frequency that makes you want to try to wake yourself from a dream ... or rather a nightmare.

Adjacent to Grand Canyon National Park is a small town called Tusayan. It is a few miles long with a strip of businesses on either side of the road that consist primarily of hotels and food establishments. As a rural area of Coconino County, law enforcement consists of Sheriff Deputies. They are lucky to have one deputy on duty and in the area at any given time. They cover a range of over sixty miles and are often not immediately available. There were no provisions at that time for fire or emergency medical service (EMS) response to the town. The National Park Service (NPS) has long had a policy of assisting its neighbors; for years Grand Canyon Rangers have responded to calls in Tusayan as if it were a satellite of the Park.

Recently, a formal memorandum of understanding was established. Prior to that, the Park responded under the heading of "it was the right thing to do." In the past, should there be a motor vehicle accident with injuries requiring extrication one mile from our entrance station, outside of our jurisdiction, and we declined to respond, the nearest EMS unit would be in Williams. The Williams responders are one hour away, if they were available, and extrication/firefighters are more than one-and-a-half hours away in Flagstaff, if they were allowed to respond.

We used our Park contract helicopters to fly daytime emergencies to the nearest hospital in Flagstaff when they were available. But at nighttime, we called the Arizona State Department of Public Safety (DPS) helicopter, coincidentally named "Ranger" (and a numerical identifier). If DPS were available, (the nearest is in Flagstaff, seventy-four miles away), they may arrive in forty-five minutes and take at least that long to return. The next closest is Kingman, Arizona, several hours away. If a helicopter were hours away, a ground ambulance would be more appropriate, should an injury occur that required surgery and/or hospitalization and definitive care.

Back then, the Grand Canyon had a clinic with wonderful family practitioner physicians, nurse practitioners and nurses. But there were no surgical facilities and no accommodations for overnight stay or critical care. They could possibly give a "clot-buster" like streptokinase to a heart attack victim at the clinic, but then the patient would have to be transported to a critical care facility in a hospital with the appropriate specialists.

On December 13, the evening had been steady with calls and responses, then quieted just before 11:00 p.m. The tone came at 10:58 p.m. It was the required emergency tone that is sounded over the air onto the rangers' radios. This gets your attention and your adrenaline rushing; a six-note "high low" tone that stops you immediately. The NPS Dispatcher, Julie, gave the call to Kent, at the time one of two Kents on the South Rim. (This Kent is married to Tammy who is a paramedic. Coincidentally, I am married to a Kent and am also a paramedic. I recall once a dispatcher telling me how she received a call for a "Kent," but the caller could not remember his last name. The caller then remembered that this particular "Kent" was married to a paramedic. The dispatcher then informed him that both Kents were married to paramedics. Thinking this must be a peculiar job qualification, the caller stated he needed to talk to the Kent who was the Fire Chief, my Kent).

Julie told Kent that there was a report of a stabbing at the Quality Inn in Tusayan, that the nearest deputy was thirty miles away, and the County was requesting our assistance. The ranger who receives the call makes the assignments. Kent requested the only other two rangers on duty, Fred and myself, to respond in the ambulance, Medic 1, while he responded directly in his patrol car. En route, Dispatch gave further details. Apparently the victim had been stabbed in the chest and the assailant was loose in the area, but possibly corralled by others. There was a Christmas party at the Quality Inn and many persons were in attendance. Kent laid out his plan on car-to-car radio as we drove the five miles to the Quality Inn. He and Fred would enter first while I held back and watched the rear. Then, if they were able to make the scene safe by apprehending the suspect and the weapon, I would change roles from Law Enforcement Ranger to Paramedic and see to the needs of the patient.

Many people don't understand the concept of scene safety priority. It is foolhardy to rush to the aid of a trapped victim in a car on a cliff without first stabilizing the vehicle. It is stupid to try and administer to an electrocution victim without first turning off the electricity. It can be downright fatal to respond to the pleas of an assault victim without knowing where the assailant is, as well as his weapon. You can't possibly help anyone if you yourself are injured or killed trying to help him or her before the scene is safe.

I arrived at Medic 1 first so took the wheel. Fred was in the passenger seat and when I heard that the stabbing was in the chest, I knew this was a "surgical disease." You need the right cure for any specific disease, such as insulin for diabetes, Valium for seizures, bronchodilators for asthmatics, and surgeons for traumas. There were no surgeons at the clinic, so I asked Fred to request Ranger 36, the DPS Paramedic helicopter out of Flagstaff, even before we arrived on scene. If it were a minor injury, we'd turn them around with an apology. But time is of the essence in severe cases.

We turned in at the Imax Theater adjacent to the Quality Inn.

We had received a description of the suspect, a Native American male about forty-five years of age with salt and pepper hair, wearing a plaid shirt and blue jeans. Fred and Kent, with their guns drawn, entered the front double glass doors of the Inn through a crowd of about forty people while I stayed at the entrance. I had my service pistol, a Sig-Sauer 9 mm semi-automatic, pulled and held along the side of my right leg. Over my shoulder was my thirty-pound EMS advanced life support pack. I looked around for the suspect, especially to the rear, not knowing where he was.

When the crowd saw me with my EMS pack, standing in the doorway, many began to shout to me to go help Tony, later identified as the victim of the stabbing. When I didn't move to enter the Inn, the crowd became more belligerent, calling to me to help. Seeing the results of scores of victims of shootings and stabbings over fifteen years as a paramedic, I knew that time was of the essence. But I also knew that I would be useless if I ran in blindly and became a victim myself. I tried to explain this to the unruly, largely intoxicated crowd and called to them to stand back as they began to approach me.

In what seemed like a very long time but, in fact, was less than a minute of our arrival, Fred came running around the corner entrance to the dining area and waved for me to go in. He said they had the suspect and I could go to the patient. I holstered and snapped in my weapon and mentally changed hats as I entered. As I rounded the corner, I saw the suspect, Harry, face down on the ground with his wrists handcuffed behind his back. He looked older than the described forty-five years and I later learned he was fifty-eight years old. He was next to a flight of stairs and Kent was straddling him, both as a measure to secure the suspect and to keep the crowd away from Harry. There was an angry, ugly atmosphere to the Christmas partyers and it wouldn't have taken much for them to take matters into their own hands. Kent pointed to a pocketknife on a shelf next to him. It didn't look threateningly large, perhaps three inches long, but you would be amazed what you can hit inside a human body with a three-inch long pocketknife. It doesn't take a butcher knife to cause a lot of damage.

I took all of this in as I turned the corner and never broke stride. On the floor was an adult male, Tony, with a single stab wound to the chest. There was blood on his shirt and on the hands of the bystanders kneeling beside him, but very little was exiting the wound. The wound was about one inch long to the left of his sternum near the fourth rib. As I knelt closer, I could see even more blood and estimated two units, about a liter, on the floor and on Tony's clothes. Tony was white as a sheet, sweaty, not moving and making incomprehensible sounds. I could tell he was breathing at about 12 times a minute but I could not feel a pulse either in the carotid artery in his neck or the radial artery in his wrist. I asked the crowd to step back and spoke to the man and woman kneeling beside Tony. They said he had been stabbed. They didn't know why Harry stabbed him, but over time Tony slowly collapsed and lost consciousness. They implored me over and over again to please help him. The odor of alcohol on their breath was strong and I asked them, too, to step back. It was not easy to pick out sober persons in the crowd.

Fred arrived with oxygen and placed a non-rebreather facemask over Tony's face. This would give him the maximum possible, almost 98% oxygen. Tony was showing textbook signs of shock.

Technically, shock is defined as inadequate tissue perfusion.

Not enough blood with its oxygen carrying capacity reaches cells. The cells suffer, then tissues, then organs, then the body as a whole. The circulatory system is closed and consists of the pump (the heart), the pipes (the blood vessels), and the fluid (the blood). Interrupt any one of these three and oxygen does not get to the cells. I couldn't tell if Tony had been stabbed in the heart and the pump was failing, or a blood vessel had been severed and he had lost so much fluid that the body had little left to circulate. Without fluid, blood pressure drops. It takes about 80 millimeters of mercury, measured as the systolic blood pressure, to get blood to the brain of a person lying down. A healthy person has a pressure of about 120/80. When the systolic blood pressure falls below 100, the brain struggles for oxygen. People with a systolic blood pressure of less than 100 go through altered levels of consciousness and eventually pass out. I've often thought that fainting is the body's attempt to get the head lower than the rest of the body so it can again receive blood and perfusion.

When the body starts to go into shock, it becomes stressed and responds with a stress reaction, often referred to as "fight or flight." Adrenaline is released, causing the heart to pump harder and faster to increase the perfusion to the cells. The lower the blood pressure, the faster the heart goes to try to compensate. The blood vessels in the periphery of the body decrease their diameter so less blood flows to the skin. This gives the skin a pale appearance. An additional stress reaction is the outpouring of sweat, called diaphoresis in the medical world. This moisture, coupled with poor skin circulation, cools the skin. A person in shock often presents with pale, cool, diaphoretic skin, and that is just how Tony appeared. That, coupled with my inability to feel a strong pulse in his neck, meant his systolic pressure had to be less than 80. This was not good.

I asked Fred to set up an IV of normal saline for me as I placed a tourniquet around Tony's left upper arm. I needed to add more fluid, fast, in an effort to circulate the few blood cells left in his body. I couldn't see a vein but I knew where it was supposed to be. One of the largest accessible veins on the arm is on the inside of the elbow in the antecubital space (AC). I used a 16-gauge catheter that had a wide opening, or bore, so fluid could go in quickly. Feeling for a slight ridge in the AC beneath my gloved fingers, I used the end of the needle to break the skin and enter the vein. Then I advanced the catheter over the needle, leaving it in the vein and pulled the needle out. I placed the needle in a sharps container for safety. I attached the end of the IV tubing that Fred handed me. I opened the fluid flow regulator wide open, handed the one-liter bag of fluid to a bystander and told him to squeeze hard on the bag to force the fluid in quickly. Fred quickly ran to the ambulance for a backboard and gurney so we could package Tony and go. He needed a surgeon, and we were trying to buy him time.

I listened to Tony's lungs with my stethoscope and could hear the "shhhsh" sound of air moving in and out. I then placed it over his heart and could not hear it beat. This was grave. Something was between my stethoscope and his heart, muting the "lub dub" sound of the valves closing. I was afraid the sac around the heart was filling with blood and was squeezing the heart so tightly that it couldn't pump well, causing the pressure to plummet.

The sac around the heart is the pericardium and when it is pushing with pressure against the heart, it's called a pericardial tamponade. A needle inserted into the sac of the heart could relieve this pressure and allow the heart to beat again. This is a straightforward procedure I was taught years ago as a paramedic in Stanislaus County, California. Take a large bore, long needle or catheter and insert it under the bottom of the sternum or breastbone. Pointing upward at a 45-degree angle, pull back on the plunger as you approach the heart and if you hit a fluid filled pericardium, the syringe would pull it out, taking the squeezing pressure off of the heart and buying the patient some time.

However, Arizona does not allow paramedics to perform this procedure so I knew getting him to a doctor was paramount, should this be the problem. Beck's triad identifies a pericardial tamponade as plummeting systolic blood pressure and rising diastolic pressure, muffled heart tones, and blood backing up in the veins bringing blood to the heart. This is most easily seen in the jugular veins of the neck as they become distended and stand out. Jugular venous distention (JVDs) is what it's called. Tony only had the muffled heart tones of the triad, no JVDs or narrowing pulse pressure.

I placed a blood pressure cuff on Tony and was amazed that I could pick it up. That was the good news. The bad news was that the systolic pressure was only 40. I was able to estimate his pulse at about 120. By this time Deputy Sheriff Glenn had arrived and took custody of the suspect, Harry. This freed Kent to come and help Fred and me. We placed Tony onto the backboard and he began to moan. That was a good sign. We strapped him down and turned to grab the gurney and found ourselves surrounded by over ten "helpful" citizens, not one of them sober. We asked them to step back and they did, at first, and then some pushed the gurney forward as we lifted the backboard supporting Tony. More reached over to push the board onto the gurney and Kent and Fred had to waste precious seconds pushing the crowd back.

When I exclaimed that he had been placed on the gurney backward, the crowd surged in and lifted Tony almost to our shoulders! We quickly turned the gurney around and again asked the crowd to move away so we could get to the ambulance. Only ten minutes had passed since we arrived at the patient's side.

As we left the dining room I saw Glenn with Harry. I don't know what prompted me to say it, just one of those gut feelings, but I turned to Deputy Glenn and said, "It looks bad and I don't know if he'll make it." Glenn's prisoner could go from an assault suspect to a murderer in a heartbeat... or lack of one.

We loaded the gurney with Tony into the back of Medic 1 and Kent jumped in with me. Fred told me that he heard the helicopter was still more than forty minutes away. I told him to take us to the clinic, less than one mile from the helibase, in case there was anything the doctors there could do while we waited for the helicopter. Kent placed the EKG electrodes onto Tony's bare chest to hook up the heart monitor. I set up a second liter of normal saline and straddled Tony's legs in the back of the ambulance to reach the AC in his right arm against the wall. Fred drove quickly but smoothly, and in a few seconds, I had the second IV established. I reached up for the tape just as I felt movement beneath me. Tony was moving his legs. Then he began to shout. He shot both arms straight up into the air, pulling out the IV in his right arm. Blood and IV fluid began to run all over as I put pressure on the IV site. Tony continued to yell, kick, and flail his arms. Kent desperately grabbed his left arm preserving that IV site and called to Tony to calm down. I sat on his legs and pulled his right arm down. The heart monitor showed a fast rhythm at 136, and his breathing was now twenty times a minute. Tony was showing signs that oxygen was indeed getting to his brain. He had gone from unconsciousness to an altered level of consciousness (ALOC). Different people react differently in the ALOC state. Some are passive, some goofy, some disoriented, some combative. Tony was combative and we suddenly had a fight on our hands.

It was a real catch-22. We wanted his blood pressure to come up to perfuse his brain, but we didn't want it up so high that he was combative. But the former was more desirable so we would deal with it. Our fluid challenge was working.

Two minutes from the clinic we heard radio traffic. There was a big fight going on at the Bright Angel Lodge and someone was hurt very badly. "We need a medic now," came the report. Kent and I just looked at each other. Dispatch knew we were otherwise occupied and, at 11:24 p.m., woke up off duty rangers to respond to the Bright Angel call.

By the time we arrived at the clinic, I had managed to restart the second IV, was still sitting on Tony and holding him down while Kent was trying to reason with him. Tony wasn't making any sense, yelling out random words and phrases. Fred opened the back door and a doctor and nurse greeted us. Together we adequately restrained Tony as we lifted the gurney out of the ambulance and wheeled it into the clinic into the small emergency room. We knew we would be putting him back into the ambulance for the short ride to the helibase, so stayed and assisted with his care.

A second doctor arrived but Tony was now a handful. We held his legs and arms. He was very strong. His blood pressure was up to 60 systolic, but I thought it must be higher with the strength he exhibited. Then Tony began to make sense with his yelling, and it wasn't good. He began to yell, "I can't breath!" I told the

Ready for flight, Grand Canyon National Park. Photo: Sean Brady.

Motor vehicle accident, Death Valley National Park. CHP photo.

Left: Hiking to Thunder River Falls for a patient with a diabetic emergency, Grand Canyon National Park.

Below: On a short-haul rope beneath a helicopter with Ranger Jim, Grand Canyon National Park.

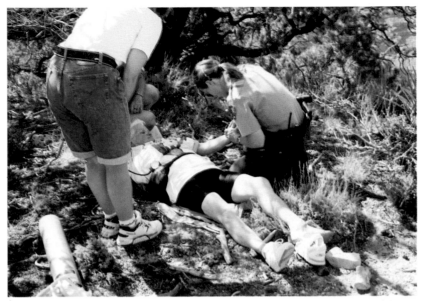

Assisting a visitor with an open ankle fracture, Grand Canyon National Park. Photo: Sheila Muleady Girardi.

Working a wildland fire with Ranger Kim, Grand Canyon National Park.

As a Structural Fire Engineer in Grand Canyon National Park. NPS photo: Mike Quinn.

Leading a structural fire entry crew, Grand Canyon National Park. NPS photo: Mike Quinn.

Fourteen-Fifty – *Hurricane Andrew Response Team members, Biscayne National Park.*

With injured fawn, Sequoia National Park.

Second Chance – *Search and rescue medical – seventeen-year-old heart attack patient, above Hamilton Lakes, Sequoia National Park.*

Death Valley Dates – *Rangers Nancy, Maya and Nancy, Death Valley National Park.*

Left: *Assisting plane crash victim, Grand Canyon Airport, Tusayan. Photo: Sheila Muleady Girardi.*

Below: The Flag *– Raising a flag over the U.S.S. Arizona Memorial, Pearl Harbor.*

On horse patrol with young visitors, Grand Canyon National Park. Photo: Sean Brady.

doctors about my concerns about a pericardial tamponade, but if that were the case, a fluid challenge would probably not have been effective, as it was apparently here. On the hope that it was something he could fix, Dr. Tom got a long cardiac needle and inserted it under the sternum at a 45-degree angle toward Tony's left shoulder. Pulling back on the plunger he looked for a return of blood. There was no return. The doctors then prepared for rapid sequence intubation, a process where Tony is put to sleep and a tube is placed in his trachea to help him breathe better. We all knew he needed a surgeon. Where was that helicopter? Hopefully, somewhere in the sky flying as fast as it could toward us.

Tony yelled two more times that he couldn't breathe and then collapsed. He went totally limp. He stopped breathing. His heart stopped. We started CPR. Advanced airway maneuvers were initiated, drugs were pushed. I reached my fingers to where his right leg met his torso to feel for a femoral pulse. There was none. CPR was being performed perfectly, and we should have been able to feel a femoral pulse with each compression of the chest, but Tony was a trauma case. There was no blood left to circulate. There was no blood left to push through the femoral artery for me to feel. There was no blood left to carry oxygen to Tony's brain. Tony died.

One of the doctors called the code (slang for code blue, the term used when a patient's heart stops and advanced cardiac life support is initiated) and pronounced Tony dead just after midnight. Tony was gone and his body was left behind. The exodus that occurs and the way the atmosphere changes when a code is called is amazing. Everyone generally leaves the room – doctors, technicians, medics, everyone. Only a lone nurse who prepares the body for transport to the morgue stays. This time everyone left and I was alone, standing there. It's strange how I feel at times like that. I can look at a body and know when "someone" is there or not. I knew Tony was gone. I looked at his traumatized body and felt helpless.

The nurses returned, quickly covered Tony and moved him out of the room. A head injury trauma patient from the fight at the Bright Angel Lodge was coming in by way of Medic 2. They needed the room. Tony didn't. He was wheeled out and gently placed behind a closed curtain. I walked into the outer hall just as the doctor was telling Tony's friend he was dead. She screamed and fell into the doctor's arms, crying and saying, "No, no, no," over and over again. He comforted her as best he could until the next patient came and he had to go.

The new patient needed an Intensive Care Unit, maybe a neurologist. The helicopter was only minutes out. It was his lucky night. He didn't have to wait forty-five minutes for the helicopter to arrive, it was here, ready for him, courtesy of Tony. They flew him south to the hospital. He lived.

It was just after midnight. We slowed down and cleaned up. I sat at the EMS desk and began the long but necessary task of documentation. They rarely show the paperwork on a television drama, but often it takes longer to do than the call itself. I was in the "traffic lane" of the clinic, right by the entry door and took time away from report writing to speak to the many persons who came in. Present were the priest, the witnesses, the other rangers, the lab tech and more. I called my husband Kent. It was good to hear him and share the tragedy of the night. Once the paperwork was done, I felt renewed. I was done with the call and could move on. I have always been able to do that, thank goodness.

Through the night and the next day the events leading up to the stabbing became clearer as I spoke to many who were there and heard the stories others had gathered. There was a Christmas party at the Quality Inn with dancing, drinking and music. Several young girls, about 12 or 13 years old, were dancing with each other to the fast and fun tunes when Harry approached them. He was apparently intoxicated and asked several of the girls to dance with him. They refused. He insisted, becoming loud and belligerent. A guest named Richard saw Harry harass the girls and told him to leave them alone. Harry told Richard to mind his own business. A small shoving match ensued and Richard, more sober and bigger than Harry, won. Harry left the dance floor and sat down next to a woman, glaring at Richard.

The woman later stated she saw Harry reach into his pocket and take out a pocketknife. He meticulously opened it, stared at the blade then looked up for Richard. Harry thought he spotted him not too far away, with his back to him. He got up and approached him. When Richard turned around, Harry stabbed him in the chest. Except it wasn't Richard. It was Tony. Tony was an innocent bystander Harry had mistaken for Richard. Tony had no clue or premonition as to what was happening and by the time he reacted, the knife was deep in his chest.

The Medical Examiner stated that an artery in Tony's chest had been cut with the knife. With every beat of Tony's heart, blood spurted from the internal artery and began filling up his chest cavity. Eventually, blood filling his thoracic cavity squeezed his heart and lungs so they could no longer expand to pump or to breathe. Though the chest was a closed cavity, Tony eventually bled to death. A thoracic trauma surgeon may have been able to crack Tony's chest, find the bleeder and stop the flow of blood, if it had happened right outside a trauma center with the surgeon available. As it was, there was no such availability in rural northern Arizona. Harry, his knife and time, all killed Tony. Before I left the clinic that early morning, I finished my paperwork and went home to sleep.

The next day I readied for my shift, which began at 4:30 p.m. I completed my exercises and had the radio on when I heard the alert tones. It was 4:58 p.m. A 911 call came in for a suicidal male, described as 45 years old with a red t-shirt and jeans, gray hair, beard and mustache. Ranger Don headed to the Maswik Hotel and I responded along with Ranger Fred. The subject, Daniel, was in the lobby. He was intoxicated, slurring his words, and stating he wanted to die. The company who runs the hotel had a Fire and Safety person on scene, Dave. Dave informed us that Daniel had been in such a rage that when he spoke on the phone prior to our arrival, he smashed the phone receiver against the phone, breaking it to pieces.

We surrounded Daniel and Fred asked him to step outside. We didn't want Daniel going ballistic in the lobby with a lot of innocent bystanders around. After much coaxing, he agreed and staggered out the front door. He was quickly taken into custody. That's a polite way of saying we arrested him. Fred placed him in handcuffs with his hands behind him, searched him, and placed him in his patrol car. We then drove to our booking facility that is a small two-room jail. Daniel broke at least two misdemeanor laws, in addition to being a troubled individual. We used those criminal acts to get him into custody as a first stage of getting him out of the public eye and to keep him from hurting himself, others, or property.

The National Park Service has a Code of Federal Regulations (CFR) that consists of misdemeanor laws. When violations of the CFR occur, the U.S. Magistrate hears them. We are also able to enforce federal felony laws and assimilate certain state laws not covered in our books. Here, 36CFR was being enforced. It is against the law to be intoxicated in such a manner that you cause damage to persons or property or are a threat to yourself, persons or property. This violation is called Under the Influence of Alcohol in a Park area (UIA). In addition, Daniel was arrested for disorderly conduct, which we shorten to DisCon. When a person is a nuisance, threat or causes jeopardy that breaches the public peace, that's DisCon. It can be as mild as using profane words in the presence of others, or as extreme as assault and battery.

At booking, Daniel was again searched and placed into a transport belt with his hands cuffed in front. He was photographed, fingerprinted, identified and a criminal history completed. As you can imagine, there was a lot of paperwork involved and I assisted Fred in the completion of booking forms while he wrote out the infractions on violation notices. Daniel had calmed down by this time so Fred took him up to the clinic to see one of the doctors and ascertain if he was truly suicidal or just drunk and stupid. This took almost an hour, but the doctor determined he did not need to go to a mental health facility and released him back to us with a clearance letter. Fred took Daniel off to jail, a three-hour round trip drive to Flagstaff, not including the work at the jail. Before they left we learned that this was Daniel's fourth DisCon in the Park.

Fred returned at 9:30 p.m. and Don, who was covering while he was gone, went home. It was just after midnight when Park

Superintendent Rob called in a suspicious juvenile to Dispatch. Apparently, a young Native American male was at the El Tovar parking lot looking into car windows. He had on "sloppy" khaki pants, sneakers and a winter coat. By the time Fred arrived, the suspect was gone.

Within five minutes, Fire and Safety Dave called in that the school's driver education vehicle with the big sign on the roof was going down the road. It was a bit late for class so Fred headed to the school and sure enough the driver's education car was not in its usual spot. We hit the streets looking for the car and Fred picked it up on a street leading to the far side of the school. He followed it in and activated his emergency lights ordering the car to stop. Fred immediately asked for backup.

Auto theft is a felony, a crime punishable by more than a year in prison. A misdemeanor is punishable by less than a year in prison. We treat all felony stops the same: get as many officers as possible to the scene, stay behind cover at your vehicle with your weapon drawn and focused on the suspect(s), and give commands from the safety of your vehicle. On television, you see cops run up to felony cars and that's a good way to get shot. In reality, when possible, we always do a felony stop by the book.

When I arrived, Fred had his shotgun out and aimed at the driver's education vehicle. Fred informed me it was a local juvenile we had all encountered before named Joey who was 16 years old. I had arrested Joey myself previously for auto burglary, criminal damage and minor consumption of alcohol. (On that call, Joey and a friend had had a lot of alcohol to drink and broke into a car to steal the stereo. When they couldn't get it out they went berserk, kicking in the dash, breaking the rear view mirror and the windshield, and slashing the interior roof and seats with a razor blade. Joey was so drunk he fell asleep inside the car he had burglarized and torn apart. On my early rounds the next morning I woke him up, got him out of the car and arrested him. I noted he had one latex glove on his hand that he had obviously worn to keep from leaving fingerprints; the other glove was on the floor of the car. When I asked him about the gloves, he said he wore them to keep his hands from getting cold. Yeah, right. (He got off that time with only juvenile probation.)

Fred used the public address (PA) on his car to give Joey orders. On command, Joey exited the car, put his hands in the air and turned around. He then staggered and began to lament, "What did I do? No one cares about me, who cares … just shoot me!" He invited us several times more to shoot him but it was obvious he was drunk. So far, we had him for felony vehicle theft and drunk driving. Finally, Joey assumed the arrest position and Fred placed him into custody. On a search of his person, Fred found a variety of school supplies in his pockets … pens, erasers, paper clips, pencils, blue award stars, felt tip markers and more. I searched the car and found similar items.

We called the Coconino County Deputy, also named Fred, who responded to NPS Booking. This time we would give the case to the County and perhaps they could make some charges stick. I met the school maintenance and security person, Andrew, who said no one was authorized to use the car and that the keys were kept in a locked drawer in a locked room in the locked school. I went with Andrew and we found evidence that Joey had burglarized the school (breaking and entering with force with the intent to commit a felony or theft), stole the car keys and stole school supplies. Matching supplies from Joey's pockets were strewn all over the floor. We could not find his father, but Joey's aunt was contacted, and Deputy Fred transported Joey to the Juvenile facility in Flagstaff. Another leisurely three-hour drive. I got home just before 3:00 a.m.

I woke up close to noon and again worked out. It always makes me feel better and the last two nights had been something. I don't know what I did after that but I do know what I thought and said just after 3:00 p.m. when my pager went off.

"Officer shot, Officer down, respond to the ambulance bay," came over the air.

"Oh God, oh no, oh, sh--." I rarely swear, and this was one of those times when it just came out.

I flew into my jumpsuit and stepped into my boots, not even bothering to tie them. I fastened my duty belt with my weapon, ran out the door and jumped into my patrol car. I heard the ambulance leave the bay, so I responded directly to Tusayan, to the Squire Inn. As I drove the five miles code 3 with lights and sirens, I picked up the gist of what had happened.

Deputy Sheriff, Corporal Jim, had stopped a van in the Squire Inn parking lot. After the driver and passenger got out, the driver pulled a gun, pointed it at Jim and pulled the trigger. Jim got his arm up and into the path of the pistol pointed at his head, deflected the bullet through his arm, and returned fire. Jim took cover as the suspect and his female companion jumped back into the van and sped from the scene. Jim then entered the Squire and called for backup. A doctor who was in the lobby gave him first aid, putting direct pressure on the wound until help came.

When Rangers Don and Chris arrived and saw that medical care was being provided on scene, they left to begin a high-speed pursuit of the suspect vehicle. The world responded. Rangers 36 and 33, DPS helicopters out of Flagstaff and Kingman, began to

respond and DPS officers, deputy sheriffs and rangers responded. It became a coordinated search for suspects who had shot a
police officer and were on the loose.

I pulled up to the Squire Inn and entered the front double
doors. The ambulance was already on scene and the first medics
were establishing an IV on Jim. As I entered the back office
area behind the front desk, I noted immediately an aura of calm
emitted by Deputy Jim himself. He was angry, he was in pain, but
he was not panicked or fearful. I knew the doctor and she filled
me in on the extent of the injuries. I didn't know how much
blood Jim had lost, but the radial and ulnar arteries were right
where he was shot, so I kept an eye out for shock in case one of
those blood vessels was damaged. Jim's vital signs, pulse, blood
pressure, skin signs, respiratory rate and lung sounds were all
pretty good. He was a bit pale and his pulse climbed into the 90s,
but for just having been shot, he was coping well. He said it hurt
like hell.

Jim needed a surgeon. It was daylight so we could use the
Park ship. I told Dispatch to inform the helibase we were en
route for the flight to Flagstaff. If there was going to be a delay,
I would go to the clinic but, when I heard the ship was ready, we
bypassed the clinic and headed for the helicopter called 210.

By that time, the initial adrenaline had worn off and Jim
really began to feel the pain. I spoke to him in the back of the
ambulance. He said after he was shot he put his gun under his left
arm pit and held his left wrist with his right hand. Later, when he
pulled his right hand away to reload, bone, bullet and watch
fragments came away in his right hand from his shattered wrist.
He had been wearing a watch, which got blown into his wrist
along with the bullet. I didn't ask him if it was still ticking ... at

least not right away. Jim was in a lot of pain and I attempted a call to the base station physician for orders but could not get through. So, I went on standing orders.

Morphine is a powerful narcotic and can often work wonders. But it also has serious side effects of respiratory depression and hypotension (below normal blood pressure). I made sure he was alert and had a good systolic blood pressure, then opened the drug kit and pulled it out, loading it into the injector. We call morphine sulfate "MS" for short. A doctor once told me that pain is the antidote for narcotics, so if there is a lot of pain, you will need a lot of MS. Don't worry too much about side effects, just keep an eye on the patient and the vital signs. I gave him three milligrams (mg) which didn't even faze Jim or the pain. In fact, the pain was getting worse as the severed tendons and ruptured muscles were now starting to spasm.

I finally got through to the base station at Flagstaff Medical Center (FMC) and they okayed my use of MS for the pain and Valium for the muscle spasms. Jim's pain was still a "10" on a severity scale of 1-10. We had loaded Jim onto the gurney in Medic 1 and placed his weapon in the locked drug cabinet. On our arrival at the helibase, there were a lot of people around to help. Park Criminal Investigator Bev came on board the ambulance as we arrived and took custody of Jim's weapon, asked him what happened, and got another thorough description of the suspects. We loaded Jim onto the gurney in the helicopter. I propped his shoulders up a bit and placed the oxygen, heart monitor and pulse oximeter where I could see and get at them. I put on my helmet, secured my seat belt and gave the pilot a thumb's up. We were ready for flight. It had been about thirty minutes since Jim had been shot.

We lifted off and headed southeast to Flagstaff. I could hear the radio traffic regarding the search for the suspect and relayed what I heard to Jim. He was still in a lot of pain and I continued to titrate the medications to help him. We finally had a moment where he could tell me what happened.

He said he was following a black 1976 Chevy van that had a note in the rear window that said, "License plate has been stolen." Jim stopped the van and a 36-year-old male named Theodore stepped out. He was 6'2" and 240 pounds, and had a female companion in the passenger seat. Jim questioned the man who cooperated with him. At one point Theodore asked permission to reach into a small backpack and get a tissue. Jim said okay, but watched him carefully. Suddenly, Theodore pulled out a large semiautomatic weapon. Jim guessed it was a 9 mm or .45 caliber gun and Theodore swung it at Jim, pulling the trigger as it rose from his chest to his head. Jim quickly raised his left arm and swept the gun from his face, but it went off on his arm. More shots went off, hitting Jim's patrol car. Jim pulled his gun and returned fire. He was not sure, but he thought he hit the suspect. Jim ran for cover toward the Squire Inn and wanted to keep the suspect from running inside and getting hostages. Jim put his gun under his armpit and reloaded, his left hand dangling uselessly. He watched as the suspect jumped into the van and sped off. Jim then entered the Inn and went behind the manager's desk and called 911.

In so many ways the story he told was unreal. It was television. But then, these last forty-one hours had been pretty unreal. The proof lay beside me in the helicopter as I took vital signs and administered meds. Jim decided that MS was a puny drug and that it was not affecting him at all. I knew then, after 15 mg of

MS and 5 mg of Valium, just how much pain he was in and how stoic he was. Anyone else would have been unconscious and I'd have been preparing to breathe for him or her. He was still alert, angry and in pain. I tried again for another radio patch to FMC but was unable to get through. I used Jim's orientation, level of consciousness, pain level, and vital signs as a guide. I finally got the pain down to a "7" when the muscle spasms began to return. I couldn't help but think of how bad it would be without any meds on board.

We arrived at FMC and landed on the concrete pad adjacent to the Emergency Room. Jim was still alert with stable vital signs so we waited for the helicopter to shut down to offload. Jim was placed in a cubicle and another officer was there to greet us and provide support for and information to Jim. I knew it was late in the day and our ability to fly would end thirty minutes past official sunset. We call that "pumpkin time." We restocked, cleaned up, and I said goodbye to Jim. By then nurses, doctors, and technicians surrounded him. I apologized for having to leave and Jim said, "No problem." He knew about pumpkin time. He also knew we cared.

As we flew back with the sunset colors beginning far off to the west, we listened intently to the radio traffic. The suspect was still at large. Later, when we heard details, we learned the suspect left the highway and went off onto dirt roads. He came across a family with a pickup truck, choosing a Christmas tree for the holidays. Theodore pulled up in the van and grabbed his female companion and threw her into the driver's seat of the family truck, holding a pistol on the startled family. The husband/dad was an off duty Phoenix police officer and felt helpless ... his own gun was in the truck Theodore was about to hijack! Then, inexplicably, the suspects got out of the truck, back into the van and sped off. The Phoenix cop ran to his truck and found his own gun was still there. He also saw blood all over the passenger seat. Theodore was bleeding, badly. Jim had hit him, and he wasn't able to drive. We later learned they abandoned the truck and returned to the van because Theodore's girlfriend did not know how to drive a stick shift! The cop drove to the nearest phone and called in the encounter. Ground troops and helicopters were now in the area, preparing to locate and contain the suspects.

A few miles on, they managed to hijack a car the female suspect could drive. But, by this time, the searchers were onto them and the helicopters were able to track them from the air and direct ground forces to them. At 4:57 p.m. we heard that the female suspect was in custody. It wasn't clear if she jumped from the truck or was told to leave. Theodore continued and the helicopter spotter reported he could see a gun being waved in their direction by the suspect. At 5:30 p.m., Theodore stopped the stolen car and ran behind a tree. Five minutes later he gave up to ground officers and was placed in custody.

We landed at the South Rim helibase six minutes later. It was a regular mystery theater listening to the developing saga. We learned that Jim's return fire amputated Theodore's right ring finger and another hit him in the right forearm. I cleaned up, did my medical report documentation, and at 6:45 p.m., went home. After all . . . it was my day off.

Epilogue

In August, Ranger Kent and I testified at the murder trial of Harry. He was found guilty of second-degree murder for the death of thirty-one-year-old Tony. Harry's lawyer stated they planned to appeal. He said that Harry slipped and accidentally stabbed Tony when he was playing with his pocketknife.

Daniel was released the next day and returned to Grand Canyon, where he continued to drink and get into trouble until he lost his job. His current whereabouts are unknown.

The juvenile, Joey, was in school the next Monday. The principal was livid at the inability of the state to keep such an obviously dangerous and antisocial person out of the school system. Joey was finally expelled two months later, but eventually was allowed to return to classes. He seemed to be keeping a low profile until rangers arrested him for crashing his vehicle one morning. He was found to be under the influence of alcohol and drugs, and taken to Juvenile Detention. Because the drug and alcohol violations did not occur while he was in school, he will be allowed to return to classes when he gets out of jail.

Theodore entered a plea bargain and never went to trial. He is in prison for the next thirty-six years (we hope) for the attempted murder of a peace officer. He stated that his reason for shooting Corporal Jim was that he was on parole and didn't want to go back to prison. Corporal Jim was off duty for two months until February, on light duty until July, then returned to full duty status. In that time he had three surgeries on his arm and had a fourth scheduled to take out the metal rod placed to stabilize the arm. He has 95% use of his left hand but the doctors don't think he'll regain full sensation. He received the Medal of Valor from the Coconino County Sheriff's Department and Officer of the Year from the Flagstaff Elks Lodge Post.

12-Lead

I love to teach, especially medical topics. Winter and spring are the times for EMT classes and refreshers. This night was the second of two airway workshops. I arrived at 6:00 p.m. to assist with the skills station. The scheduled instructor failed to show so we punted. I stepped in and lectured, Ranger Paramedic Tammy coordinated the skills stations and it all went off smoothly. The twenty-four students were all very enthusiastic and sharp. We paired them up and began to rotate them through their stations. I set up a scenario and the students used a mannequin to practice their newly learned airway maneuvers. In the kitchen they practiced suctioning up horrible looking concoctions in the sink, simulated to look like emesis or vomit. Thank goodness the concoctions didn't have the smell of reality.

I was on night shift duty and had my radio on with the earphone plugged in. Just after 8:00 p.m., the EMS alert tone sounded. I dashed down the hall and grabbed my jacket as I called to Tammy that I had to leave. The call was for a 65-year-old female complaining of chest pain in the Yavapai East building.

Tammy's husband Kent was also on duty and went directly to the scene in his patrol car. As I left the Albright Training Center for my vehicle, I was hit in the face with something I didn't expect... snow! Big flakes were twirling sideways and downward and I began a careful walk to my car over the slick cement.

In my headlights through the darkness, the snow looked twice as heavy as it really was. I drove across the street to Station 1 and went in the side door to the ambulance, Medic 1. I pulled out the ambulance and closed the door behind me while the Dispatcher, Karyn, gave me a patient update. The patient was awake and alert and had shortness of breath which was now gone, but the chest pain was still there. I was en route with lights and minimal sirens (as a courtesy to the residents). I heard Kent call that he was on scene and, as I pulled up to the Yavapai, he asked for the usual ACLS (advanced cardiac life support) items. Ranger Paul also heard the call and arrived as I was entering the building. By some miracle, the patient was on the bottom floor of the two-story hotel complex – a rare event, indeed.

As I entered the hall, an elderly man held the door open and motioned to me. I later learned he was the patient's husband, Bart. He was 69, tall with a medium build and looked worried and frail. I entered with the heart monitor, pulse oximeter and drug bag. The patient was a 65-year-old female, also of medium build who was lying clothed on the hotel room bed, propped up by two pillows in a semi-sitting position. On her right side, kneeling on the floor was Kent. He had just finished placing her on oxygen and was getting a brief history. The patient's name was June. She was pale but alert. She immediately struck me as stoic, which is often a dangerous thing to be as a patient. Stoic patients are big on denial and never really want to tell you just how bad things are. I introduced myself, asked her some orientation questions, and then asked her about her chest pain. It was a dull pain just behind the lower part of her sternum with some pressure associated. It radiated up to her left armpit and down her arm to her elbow.

While every chest discomfort is treated seriously, when you get the symptoms she described, bells and whistles should go off. This could be an MI. In these cases, time is muscle. The longer the duration of chest pain, the more heart muscle is being compromised. Pain and pressure are signs of lack of oxygen, called ischemia. As it progresses, muscle goes from ischemia to injury to infarct. If you can get oxygen to the heart muscle in the stages before infarct, the muscle is not irreversibly damaged and can often repair. At infarct, there is no return. Dead heart muscle cells burst and release their cellular contents, including positively charged potassium ions. Within twenty-four hours, enzymes are released by the body to digest and remove the shattered remains of the dead tissue. Scar tissue replaces it. Scar tissue cannot contract and beat like heart muscle. The bigger the infarct, the bigger the loss of heart muscle, and the weaker the heart will be post recovery. This plays a big part in quality of life.

A small infarct will cause a patient to be judicious and careful in their everyday living, but for the most part they can live a fairly normal life. A large infarct could mean little blood is pumped through the system. People who survive have only a partial pump, get short of breath and cannot engage in strenuous activities. Some have fluids back up into their lungs, causing congestive heart failure. It's an effort just to walk to the bathroom!

Time is muscle, and I wanted to save as much as I could so June could have a good quality of life after this crisis. She also had to make it through this crisis.

I explained to June that I was concerned about her heart and that I wanted to treat her and get her to the Clinic. She agreed immediately. This was another warning sign. The patient didn't argue and didn't worry about the expense. She was past denial. She knew ... and trust me, patients know when things are serious. When a patient tells me they are going to die, I believe them. They often go into full arrest (go unconscious and their heart stops) shortly after telling me this. When patients have a feeling of impending doom, I have learned to take them very seriously. Unfortunately, they are rarely wrong. I asked Kent to start an IV of normal saline and Paul to get her vital signs. I would get her 12-lead.

Heart patients today have a vast arsenal of technology available to them. A lot of it is making its way to pre-hospital care ... to the field medics, to save time, to save muscle. We routinely place patients on a heart monitor to record their electrocardiogram, referred to as an EKG. EKG pads with conductive gel are placed on the torso and wire leads are attached to the monitor.

As heart muscle contracts, it does so in a complicated and usually, highly coordinated fashion. Negatively and positively charged atoms called ions rush in and out of each cell, polarizing and repolarizing as the events involving conduction of signals and contractions take place. This rush of ions creates an electric current that can be picked up by the heart monitor. The known, normal sequence of events starts with the filling of the top two chambers of the heart, called the atria, and progresses with atrial contraction, pushing blood through valves to the lower chambers of the heart, called ventricles. The ventricles then contract in unison and the blood passes through valves to travel through the body to deliver oxygen and pick up carbon dioxide as waste, and also travels next door to the lungs to exchange the carbon dioxide for oxygen. This is all coordinated through an electrical conduction system found throughout the heart. Without this coordinated effort, each individual heart muscle would beat at its own pace and the heart would merely quiver like a bowl of gelatin. This is called fibrillation and most often leads to death

One EKG pad is placed near or on the right arm at the torso. The second is placed on the left side in similar fashion. The third is placed on the lower left side of the rib cage below the level of the heart. This allows us to take an electric look at a "slice" through the "heart of the heart." This gives us the basic rhythm and can tell us if any dangerous electric beats are escaping the normal routine and threatening to cause the rest of the heart to mutiny, resulting in fibrillation. With three pads we can look across the top of the heart and down the side and through the middle. Three different looks or three leads. With more pads and more lead wires correctly placed, a finer cross-sectional look through the heart can be seen and details picked up.

The professional standard is the 12-lead, and is usually performed in the emergency room or Intensive Care Unit with an expensive and sophisticated machine. An experienced clinician can look at the electric cross-sections of the heart and more readily tell if tissue is being injured or infarcting. They can also tell where in the heart it is occurring. During infarction, the rupture of the cells and surge of positive potassium ions can show up as an elevation of the electric line tracing on the EKG. Dead tissue and scar tissue will block the flow of the electric current. This diversion can be seen as a deviation in the path of the electric tracing as it bounces off the non-conductive tissue and flows out in a different direction. The 12-lead can also pick up Q waves. A Q wave is a sign of infarction: a dip in the electric line like a "V" that will be there for the life of the damaged heart. A 12-lead with a Q wave in the trace is a sign that a person had an MI in the past. A Q wave with an elevation of the EKG trace showing potassium ions being released by dead cells means the heart attack is happening right now!

There is so much to the interpretation of a 12-lead. I was fortunate to go through a class a long time ago, but had little chance to use it. Now that 12-lead is approved for paramedics to use in the field, it can be a lifesaver. The EMS Coordinator recently arranged for the Park to purchase a new 12-lead heart monitor/defibrillator at over \$15,000! The Park's paramedics had a course in its use and interpretation recently and I had practiced on many of my fellow rangers and colleagues.

June would be my first real patient. The diagnosis of an MI in the field meant that the clot-buster thrombolytics could get to the patient much sooner, often saving over an hour in the process. Time is muscle. Many heart attacks, or MIs, occur when a piece of plaque breaks off and begins to block one of the coronary arteries. As time progresses, the blood products that form a blood clot also accumulate, making the clot (or thrombosis) bigger and eventually shutting off the flow of oxygen-carrying blood to the tissue beyond the clot. This can result in the ischemic tissue crying out in pain as it gets low on oxygen, becomes injured, and eventually dies. The sooner a thrombolytic drug can be given, the sooner blood can flow to the tissue beyond and save muscle. Even more modern technology is moving toward heart catheterization.

We don't carry thrombolytics in the field or do heart catheterizations, but we can buy the patient time. It's one thing to diagnose an MI, it's another to do something about it. Not all MIs are caused by clots and not all patients are candidates for thrombolytics. A narrowed, plaque-filled artery that is in spasm or is finally closed off by plaque alone will not benefit from clot-busters. That artery needs to be bypassed or cleaned out, requiring open-heart surgery or angioplasty. Nitroglycerin can dilate blood vessels with the hope that an artery in spasm or not totally blocked will get larger and allow blood through. When it doesn't work, we move on to the more powerful narcotic, morphine sulfate. Morphine, like "nitro," lowers blood pressure in all vessels, not just coronary arteries. Not only will it dilate blood vessels, it will also lower anxiety and reduce pain. By lowering anxiety, the patient calms, the heart doesn't beat as fast, and less oxygen is needed, saving muscle. Of course, the number one drug of choice is oxygen. That is the first drug given to the patient.

As Paul took June's blood pressure, she lay very still and silent. He told me her blood pressure was 180/140 (which was too high; normal blood pressure is 120/80). Her pulse was 128. Her lungs were clear. I placed the four limb leads on June, two on her upper arm and two on her legs above the ankles. Then I placed the other six leads across her chest. Using several electrodes twice allowed us to obtain a 12-lead. I placed my finger on the notch at the top of her sternum and slid to her right to the first space between her ribs. I counted down and placed a pad on the fourth space, then one across from it on her left side. I went to the fifth space and slid to a point midway across her chest, in line with her clavicle, or collarbone. This was on the edge of her breast. This was no time for being embarrassed. I moved her breast out of the way and placed a lead pad there, then one between it and the previous pad. Then I placed one to the side of her chest in line with the front of her armpit, or axillary. The last pad was adjacent, mid-axillary. I pushed the button on the monitor for 12-lead and the machine immediately beeped and flashed, "Attach EKG Leads." It's one thing to put it on the patient, but you have to remember to connect her to the monitor. That quickly accomplished, the machine began to acquire and analyze the data and, in short order, began to spit out a perfect 12-lead EKG.

As I began my systematic interpretation of the results, I noted June's husband, Bart begin to pace the room. He was worried, too. On the 12-lead, I immediately began to see signs of an MI in several of the leads. I unplugged the telephone line from the phone in the hopes of transmitting the 12-lead to our base station hospital, FMC, in Flagstaff, but the phone was not working. I typed June's name in the monitor index and reached for the nitroglycerin. An IV was established in her left arm. Kent gave her the nitro and began to load June onto the gurney. We rechecked her blood pressure and there was no change. Also, there was no change in her chest pain/pressure. The pulse oximeter on her finger said her blood was 92% saturated with oxygen ... a good sign under the circumstances. I began a radio patch to the doctor at FMC and handed Kent the aspirin and a second nitro tablet. Aspirin is remarkable. It has minor anti-clotting properties and is known to greatly increase survival in MI patients. Kent gave her the meds and we started out of the room. I stopped to ask Bart if he was okay. He said yes, that he was just worried. I asked him if he had any health problems. He admitted he'd had several heart attacks himself in the past and had bypass surgery. He denied having any current chest pain, but I turned to Paul and asked him to make sure Bart rode in the front of the ambulance where he could keep an eye on him. Bart said he was okay and joined us as we wheeled June out of the room, into the night air and snow.

In the ambulance, Paul took another blood pressure reading and, again, no change. June said her chest discomfort was the same, still radiating down to her elbow. I gave her the first of a lot of morphine she would receive that night. She told me she had a history of hypertension (high blood pressure) and a heart murmur during her pregnancies. Otherwise, she had been healthy most of her life. I rechecked her blood pressure. It was coming down, but there was still no change in her chest pain. I gave her another 2 mg of morphine. She was not short of breath and remained alert, but I could only drop her pain slightly. I use a 0-10 scale, with 10 being the worst pain. Hers started at a "5" and was now just a little less than a "4." I wanted it to be zero. Her heart was pleading for relief.

By the time we arrived at the clinic, her pressure was down to 140/100. This was a big help, but her chest pain persisted. We pulled the gurney out of the medic and wheeled her into the small, one-bed emergency room. Marchelle was the RN on call and greeted us at the door. I gave her a report and she understood the gravity of the situation and went to work. Within minutes Dr. Tom arrived and they began to make plans to give June thrombolytics. The doctors at the clinic often consult with physicians at FMC. I told Tom I could transmit June's 12-lead to FMC with our new machine. He enthusiastically agreed and I left the ER to do just that.

While others were cleaning up the equipment, I went to get the heart monitor. I then looked at Bart, who was standing next to the drinking fountain. I did not like what I saw.

Bart was pale and shaky and appeared to be making an effort to breathe. I walked over to him and could hear him wheezing. When I asked him how he was, he said he was short of breath. I helped him to a chair and asked for a stethoscope. Bart's pulse was irregular. Paul handed me a stethoscope and, as I listened, I could hear the gurgling sound of fluid in his lungs. Bart was in congestive heart failure (CHF) and was drowning in his own fluids. Paul immediately brought me oxygen and went to get the heart monitor. I placed Bart on a non-rebreather mask (one with an oxygen reservoir) to give him the maximum oxygen possible. His available surface area of lung tissue was limited and I wanted to maximize his oxygenation. Kent went to tell Dr. Tom and get an IV set up. Dr. Tom asked if we could continue with Bart's patient care because they had their hands full with June, and Kent said yes. Marchelle called another nurse at home and asked her to come in.

By this time I was getting proficient with 12-lead placements and had it on in seconds. Paul reported that Bart's blood pressure was 210/130. Here we go again. The IV was established and Lu Ann, the nurse Marchelle had called, arrived at the clinic. Bart had a history of three MIs ... all of them silent. Silent MIs are heart attacks without chest pain, and he had no chest pain now. He spoke in short, four- to five-word sentences because of his shortness of breath. He also told me he had three other bouts with CHF and a history of hypertension. His EKG showed several things: he was in atrial fibrillation (the top of his heart was quivering), a condition for which he was being treated; it showed lots of Q waves that appeared old; and it showed his enlarged heart. He was a mess. His heart was so badly damaged that it could not pump efficiently and fluids were backing up into his lungs. I gave Dr. Tom the report and he ordered Procardia and Lasix.

Procardia, also known as nifidepine, was to help lower his blood pressure. Lasix is a diuretic. It makes the kidneys work overtime. The thought is if you pee a lot, there is less fluid in your body to back up into your lungs to drown you. When I first started as a paramedic, they still used rotating tourniquets. A tourniquet was placed on three of four limbs, say, two legs and an arm. After a period of time, it would be loosened and rotated. The principal was the same: to trap fluids in legs and arms to keep it away from the lungs. But when the trapped fluid was finally released, it brought with it a lot of carbon dioxide, the fluid itself and waste products that often made the patient's condition worse.

The technician Gary had arrived to do the blood work on June and slipped over to X-ray to help Bart. Dr. Tom had ordered a chest x-ray. When it was done, we put him in a bed adjoining June's and he was hooked up to the clinic's backup heart monitor. I went to the clinic phone, plugged the phone line into the modem on the monitor, and transmitted both June's and Bart's 12-lead EKGs to FMC. Dr. Tom consulted with the doctors who were reading the transmitted EKGs and soon began administering the clot-busters to June. We again went through the clean up routine, replacing supplies and cleaning the ambulance. I finally sat down to do paperwork when Dr. Tom called me into X-ray. I'm not a doctor, but I've seen a lot of x-rays and I was just blown away when I saw Bart's. There were white, spider web-like strings all over his chest cavity with some heavy areas of whitening. All of the white represented fluid, and Bart was full of fluid. In addition, his heart was greatly enlarged, expanding across his rib cage to within an inch of the inner left margin. It was so big and inefficient, it was a wonder he was doing so well. Being at an elevation of 7,000 feet certainly wasn't helping.

In a short time, the ambulance from Williams arrived and the attendants were surprised to hear there were two patients to go. Carefully, June and Bart were placed in the back, side by side for the one-and-a-half-hour ride to FMC in Flagstaff. I held their hands and wished them luck, and then they were gone. I sat down and finished my paperwork.

Epilogue

I learned a long time ago that if you don't want to know the answer to a question, don't ask it in the first place. I've called too many times about patients I've treated only to find they later died. I rarely call now. I last saw them alive and that is usually good enough for me. But it seemed only right to follow up on June and Bart. I waited two days and called the FMC hospital operator. She confirmed that both June and Bart were still patients at FMC and that June was in the Cardiac Care Unit (CCU). I asked to speak to her nurse.

Her nurse said she was stable. Her enzymes weren't too high so there wasn't a huge amount of infarct for the body to clean up. However, since she did have an MI, they planned to do tests to check her coronary arteries. So far, other tests pointed to at least one artery being 90% blocked. Most people don't realize that heart disease is the number one killer of women. After menopause, women don't have their natural hormones, such as estrogen, which play a huge part in preventing fat and plaque build-up in arteries. After menopause, the number of incidents of MIs in women skyrockets, even exceeding men in some age categories.

As for Bart, he was much better and was out of CCU. He could be discharged, but he had no place to go, so he was still in the hospital. His daughter would be by so they could make plans to discharge him. Depending on June's tests and treatments, she would be discharged within a week or so.

Stone Creek

I was flight medic that day and had just helped evacuate a man from the mule corrals at Indian Garden. Ranger Chuck had called it in and could not put his finger on the problem. On my arrival, the man's demeanor, disposition and behavior all pointed to someone who didn't have all of his oars in the water, an emotionally disturbed person. He was flown out and taken to the Grand Canyon Clinic for evaluation. Not the most challenging call, and I later made a comment to that effect to the Helibase crew ... one I would live to regret. While we don't cause things to happen, there are some superstitions among rescuers in emergency services. You don't say the word "quiet" when it is, you don't say that you're "bored" when you are, and you don't wish for a "juicy" call if the last one wasn't, because that guarantees all hell will break loose. Just before 4:00 p.m., my comment came back to haunt me.

NPS Dispatch reported to Ranger Patrick, the Search and Rescue (SAR) shift coordinator of the day, a "serious" medical at River Mile (RM) 132. That was all of the information they had.

Patrick asked me to report to the helibase and assigned Parkmedic Steven to go with me. The call sounded ominous and benign at the same time. There is little communication from the Colorado River to the outside world because of the high canyon walls. Our River Rangers check in at pre-assigned places where they know they can reach a radio repeater on land, which are few and far between. They may be days from radio contact. On the other hand, when the President or other VIPs go down the river, the Secret Service takes $10,000 satellite telephones to communicate. They may only be minutes from reaching a satellite for communication and have the means and technology to do so fairly quickly.

The average private boat trip used to have no such capabilities and would have to wait hours or days for someone with communications equipment to come by if they were in need of help. Commercial raft trips, on the other hand, had ground-to-air radios. In an emergency, they take the radio out of its water-protective case and go to the highest point of land they can reasonably reach. They wait for a jet airliner to fly by, sometimes at an altitude of 30,000 feet over the narrow spaces between canyon walls. As soon as it is spotted, the river guides transmit like mad, as the window of opportunity to hit the airliner is limited. With minimal detail, they call frantically for help. The guides have little feedback and so hope the call has been received. They may try several times to "hit" jets as they fly over, hoping to get their urgent message out to one.

Should the airplane receive the call, they radio to the nearest major airport, usually, LAX (Los Angeles International). The tower at LAX then calls the FAA (Federal Aviation Administration) who calls the NPS (National Park Service) and the call is finally given to the SAR shift ranger at Grand Canyon. By the time they get it, any kind of lengthy message is corrupted. Rangers are lucky to get the gist of the message; in this case, the location, "River Mile 132," and the situation, "serious medical."

The river mileage begins below Glen Canyon Dam at Lee's Ferry, at RM 0 and continues west. Eight miles down is Badger Rapids; 88 miles down is Phantom Ranch; 226 miles down is Diamond Creek, where most boat trips exit the river; and 279 miles down is Lake Mead, the end of the modern Colorado River in Grand Canyon. River Mile 132 was just below Specter, Bedrock and Dubendorff Rapids on the river, and at the confluence of Stone Creek. Located on the north side of the river, Stone Creek is a popular side hike for people on boat trips who want to walk to waterfalls.

With the potential for trauma from the rapids as well as Stone Creek, the words "serious medical" left a lot open for interpretation. Added to those possibilities snakebite, anaphylactic shock from a bee sting, heart attack, and more, it was potluck as to what was really going on. I have been called to river mile rescues with little information and have had a range of situations on arrival. From stubbed toes (yes, can you believe it? … sigh) to persons who have died. There was a situation a few years ago when a river guide was climbing a wall after supper and fell and hit his head, causing intracranial bleeding. They called for help but before help could come, a doctor on the trip realized the guide would die because the swelling in his skull was building up so much pressure, it was pushing the brain through the only available hole, the one-inch opening at the base of the skull called the foramen magnum. To relieve the pressure, the doctor took the drill carried for repairs on the boat and drilled a burr hole in the skull of the unconscious river guide to relieve the pressure! Despite these efforts, the guide died. Who knew what awaited us.

We put all possibly needed equipment on the helicopter, a NOTAR (no tail rotor) MD 900, with Eric as the helispot manager and Eddie as the pilot. The helicopter, designated "210," was new to the rescue scene at Grand Canyon, and it would only be my second flight in it. Painted black and yellow like a bumblebee, 210 had two motors. It was uncomfortable for rescuers, had no set up for patient care, no insulation, was much louder inside than the old Bell Long Ranger, and was twice as expensive to run! However, this particular ship was a Park effort to commit to silent technology by example. In theory, it was quieter at a distance, and was much faster, but those things didn't make up for the difficulty in caring for a patient. You do the best you can with what you've got.

Our pilot Eddie sat in the front right seat; Eric was in the front left on the radio; and Steven and I sat in the back for the flight from the South Rim to RM 132. There had been a pre-flight meeting discussing the mission and I knew there were LZs at the delta of Stone Creek. Otherwise, there were some sheer walls up and downstream of RM 132. We were prepared mentally for hiking some distance to the patient. Because the helicopter radio does not work while in the canyon, we have a one-hour on scene protocol of checking in. Ready or not, 210 would have to fly up and out of the canyon with or without us, after one hour of being out of communication contact. If 210 didn't do that, the assumption was that we were not capable of flying out or that 210 had crashed and a second ship would be sent in to rescue the rescuers. Aaah ... rural medicine.

By the time we arrived at Stone Creek delta, it was after 5:00 p.m. It was warm-to-hot on this mid-June day and, as we dropped down into the canyon, we could tell it was getting warmer, despite the air conditioning in the ship. We started a few miles upstream of Stone Creek confluence, looking for boats and frantically waving people. The sheer black cliffs of the canyon on either side were massive, imposing and beautiful. Below, the green Colorado River was a testament to lack of recent rainfall that washes mud from the side canyons into the water to give it its muddy, red look and historical name, Colorado. Past Specter and Dubendorff, we saw some boats and people who just looked up or casually waved. None seemed to urge us toward them. As the canyon opened up and we approached Stone Creek, a curious site appeared: the most organized rescue cue I have ever had the pleasure of seeing. In unison, about twenty people on the beach stood and pushed their arms forward, all pointing upstream into Stone Creek. In that instant, we knew it was not a river related accident, but something upland, away from the river.

We flew into the side canyon, climbing, and within a short distance, saw a group of people huddled around a person lying on the ground. Above them a bright, orange cross was laid out on the hillside, leaving no doubt that this was the spot. We hovered near the group for just an instant and saw no LZs near by, so we went upstream. There, on the edge of a cliff, was a slanting rock too severe to stay for any length of time or to place a patient on, but it did meet our criteria for off-loading me. We are not allowed to do one skid landings or jump from helicopters any-more (both of which I have done, but a long time ago). Here Eddie landed the ship on both skids and held power to keep us from slipping off the ledge. I off-loaded with only my EMS pack to get to the patient as quickly as possible. Steven, Eric and Eddie would look for a better LZ and bring the rest of the needed supplies. With the rotor turning above me, I was pummeled in downdraft as I stepped out of 210 and onto the slanted rock. The steep angle of the rock and Eddie's ability to keep the helicopter from slipping off truly impressed me. With my flight helmet still on, I grabbed my bag and crawled forward under a rock where Eddie could see me. I gave him a thumbs up. He nodded and 210 slid off the rock and into the gorge, lifting up, soaring and circling the canyon to find a better LZ.

I stood and began taking my helmet and nomex flight gloves off. The terrain was desert-like with no trees, few shrubs and lots of rock and dirt. I stepped onto a well-worn trail where a man, identifying himself as a doctor, approached me and asked if I had IV set ups. I said yes and everything else we would need. I asked him why I was called. He said that a woman was suffering from chest pain and needed help. I immediately relaxed. A heart attack was pretty easy to stabilize. I told him not to worry; I had a heart monitor with EKG capabilities and heart medication. We turned to walk the hundred or so yards to the patient and I called on the line of sight channel on the radio to 210 to tell them it looked like an MI. I asked the doctor when the chest pain started. He said it started about 2:15 p.m. when the 43-year-old patient, Teresa, fell off a forty-five foot cliff onto her chest and back, hitting a shelf on the way down. I stopped, momentarily stunned by the instant change in the patient's mechanism of injury. I called the ship, correcting the call from a medical to a trauma, and knew that time would be of the essence. While I might be able to stabilize a MI patient in the field, a trauma patient would need a surgeon. We try to get trauma patients to surgeons within one hour of injury, calling that the Golden Hour, knowing that most serious trauma patients don't last beyond that time. This had been over three hours and most people don't survive forty-five-foot falls, let alone the hour after the event. When I arrived at the patient, Teresa, my gut told me this was bad.

I could tell she was awake because she was gritting her teeth. Her face was pale and she was immobilized by a variety of handy items accessible to the boat crew. Clean disposable baby diapers, of all things, padded her head and an orange life vest was roped across her chest. She was covered by a blue tarp and tied to a metal backboard that a private trip had donated. There were twigs and leaves caught in her hair and she was covered with dirt from the fall. As I knelt down on her right side I was told she had "major pain in her chest" and could not move her legs. I looked up at the reporting voice and was introduced to Peg, one of the river guides. She had a series of papers and had been marking Teresa's progress on them over the past few hours. She gave me brief details of the accident, and later I learned more of the story.

Teresa was on a commercial river trip that had stopped for a side hike to some waterfalls on Stone Creek. One witness stated Teresa was an avid photographer and wanted to do the optional five-hour hike up Stone Creek on her own, going at a leisurely pace to take pictures. In the witness statements that were later gathered, one couple looked up the trail toward the falls when they heard gravel rolling. They witnessed the beginning of Teresa's fall from the trail edge. She was in a "layout" position at first, hitting the back of her neck on a ledge about fifteen feet down. Then she flipped completely over in mid-air and dropped out of sight. Another witness saw Teresa yelling after she hit the ledge, and watched as she continued a vertical fall of thirty feet into the rocks and bushes below. The witness began calling for help and one of the river guides, Rachel, climbed down to Teresa.

As an EMT, Rachel knew not to move Teresa, assessed her airway, and began calling to others for additional help. Persons began running down the trail for medical supplies, technical rescue equipment, and extra personnel. Rachel called to them to unpack the radio and begin the call for help. Rachel later stated that they packaged Teresa, protecting her spinal column from further injury, and with the help of over twenty-five people, used ropes to raise her up the waterfall to the trail, where she was put in a safe area, awaiting our arrival. Rachel stated that it did not appear that Teresa had lost consciousness and was alert the whole time. Another witness stated Teresa was conscious but groggy during the carry out. Peg added that Teresa, herself, was a doctor.

I radioed to 210 the equipment needed and introduced myself to Teresa. Her vital signs were not encouraging. She was having difficulty breathing, at a rate of 40 - 45 (normal is 12-16), her pulse was 120 (normal is 60 - 80), and her blood pressure 100/60 (normal is 120/80). Somewhere the boat crew had obtained an open neck cervical spine collar to protect her neck and a back board and had done a super job of immobilizing Teresa. I just couldn't get at her torso with the life vest in the way. When Steven arrived I asked him to remove it after initiating oxygen therapy. I set up a liter of normal saline IV solution and started a large bore size 16-gauge catheter in her right hand. She didn't flinch as I pierced her pale hand with the needle, advancing it slightly and threading the plastic catheter into her vein. After drawing blood, I opened up the IV to give her fluids to buy her time.

From the beginning of my contact I had been talking to Teresa. She was oriented, knowing who she was, where she was, the time and what had happened to her. She stated that she had merely slipped and fallen, denying any dizziness or fainting prior to the fall. She was in good health, taking only one medication with no significant past medical history. I asked her what kind of a doctor she was, and she told me she was a surgeon. I knew then that Teresa knew what was going on with her and decided to share all of my findings with her. I also realized that for anyone to make it through thirteen years of medical school and surgical residency she had to have a hell of a mental constitution. I hoped it still existed within her while her body was falling apart.

She complained of extreme pain in her chest and in her right upper back area. I assessed her head and found no great trauma. She did not open her eyes spontaneously. Her complexion remained pale and though she had numerous scrapes and cuts, her head was largely unscathed.

As I cut the life vest straps on my side of Teresa's body, she moaned in pain. Someone from the surrounding crowd asked me if I could give her something for the pain. Rather than enter into a long discussion about the dangers of giving pain medication to persons with multisystem trauma – how it lowers their blood pressure and diminishes their drive to breathe – I merely replied that I did have morphine. I listened to her lungs and noted I could hear air going into both sides, but not much and not very deeply. Steven had placed her on oxygen by nasal cannula at six liters per minute because we had limited supplies. I placed her on the heart monitor and was pleased to tell Teresa that her EKG looked good; that her heart tones were clear and not muffled. I also noted her neck veins were flat, also a good sign. Increased pressure in her chest from damaged heart or lungs could make the external jugular veins distend (JVD), so no JVD was a good sign.

Her rib cage, on the other hand, was a mess. It was distorted and stair-stepped in appearance on both sides in different places, moving contrary to adjacent ribs. She had multiple broken ribs causing a flail chest and ineffective breathing and air exchange. From below her umbilicus and hips, she could feel nothing. She could not move her legs nor feel me touch her hips, legs, feet or toes. She had good pulses to her feet, which I marked after I asked a bystander to remove Teresa's hiking boots and socks. I ran my pen along the bottom of both feet in to her big toe and watched as her toes curled down. Her superficial plantar reflex was intact, but communication from her lower spine had stopped from her waist and below. Teresa knew that the lack of motion and sensation below her waist could be dire, but I told her, "Let's hope it was just swelling on the spinal cord that will go away." As I stood up to prepare to move her, I saw how small and vulnerable she looked. Despite her background, she was scared and in pain, and there was no family with her on this trip. We would be all she had at this critical time.

Though it seemed a long time, it had been only six minutes since my arrival at Teresa's side. We began to carry her to the helicopter about a quarter mile away. Time was her enemy and we needed to get her to definitive care. At 210, we put Teresa in with her head forward, because the ship would tilt down while in flight. I'd rather have blood run to her head and brain where she needed it than to her toes. Extra equipment was piled around the helicopter and secured. The backboard we had brought pressed against the door to Teresa's right. I listened again to Teresa's lungs but the sounds were diminished with not as much air going in. I placed her on a pulse oximeter, which measured the oxygen saturation to her tissues, and it was 97%. Still good. I sat in a seat adjacent to her head and Steven was near her legs. I asked him to set up and start a second IV en route. We lifted off shortly after 5:30 p.m. I told Eddie we were to go to FMC and not to the Grand Canyon Clinic. He said that he didn't have enough fuel but that he could stop at the contract helicopter's home base and refuel without shutting down.

I asked for a radio patch through EMSCOM to talk to the Base Station Physician. I wanted to give Teresa high-dose SoluMedrol, new to pre-hospital care. While not a cure, in cases of traumatic paralysis, it can reduce the swelling on the spine at the point of injury to buy some more function or feeling if, indeed, swelling is the culprit. It has its drawbacks though. Steroids can depress the immune system and I knew with Teresa's chest injuries she would likely develop pneumonia and would need her immune system. I would let the base station physician make the call.

As I waited to get through, Teresa complained that the pain in her chest was increasing. Her blood pressure was down to 88/p, meaning I palpated it rather than heard it (it's too loud to hear through a stethoscope in a helicopter). Because the helicopter was not designed to carry patients, the backboard sat on four hollow plastic pieces raising the backboard only three inches off the floor. Steven and I bent over to take care of Teresa and he had a heck of a time starting the second IV. Finally, it was established. I then gave up on trying to establish a phone patch through the EMSCOM system and went through the Park radio system. The doctor on duty okayed the SoluMedrol and 2 liters of IV fluids. She was also concerned about the chest trauma and the diminished breath sounds. Teresa was bleeding internally into her chest cavity and possibly into her abdomen, as the skin in her upper abdomen was getting tighter. I also had to watch for a tension pneumothorax.

The lungs in the chest are like two balloons in individual boxes. As the box expands with each breath, it pulls the balloon with it, creating a negative pressure and air rushes in from the mouth or nose to fill this balloon. If there is a hole in the balloon, the chest still expands, but less air goes in, rushing through the hole and into the box. As long as the air can go back through the balloon and out of the mouth, you merely have to deal with a collapsed lung or simple pneumothorax. However, if the air cannot get back through the hole, it acts like a one-way valve to cause air to build up in the box. With each breath, the amount of air in the box increases and has no place to go. Soon it collapses the lung, pushes the heart to the side, and tries to collapse the other lung in its box. This is called a tension pneumothorax. It causes the trachea to slide sideways and the neck veins to stand up (JVD). Soon the patient is gasping for breath and the heart stops from the pressure on it, causing death.

The answer is to put a chest tube into the box or thorax, allowing the air a way out. We don't put chest tubes in, but we can perform a needle thoracostomy. A large bore needle is placed in the second intercostal space, just over the rib to avoid major arteries, midline with the clavicle, or collarbone, and into the thorax. The air rushes out and, instead of a tension pneumothorax, we have an open pneumothorax. Not great, but survivable. An unrelieved tension pneumothorax is certain death.

As Teresa's oxygen saturation dipped to 92%, we landed in the town of Tusayan, just outside of the park. The door next to Teresa was flung open and the extraneous supplies thrown off. I barely looked up. Within minutes, we were airborne, en route to FMC. I had never been in a helicopter when it had been refueled, let alone when it was a hot refuel (with the motor still going and the rotors still turning). It's not the safest practice in the world and is forbidden except under extraordinary circumstances. That is what existed now. To do it by the book would have cost us perhaps twenty minutes – minutes that Teresa couldn't spare.

Steven opened the drug bag and took out the vials of powdered SoluMedrol. We mixed it with sterile water. I had him carefully inject 16 cc into each of two vials and gently mix them. Then I worked out the math. The dose is 30 mg per kg of body weight. I guessed Teresa at about 140 pounds, or 65 kg. I calculated 30 x 65 is 1950, or about 2000 mg of medication to be given over thirty minutes. With 32 cc of fluid, that meant a bit more than a cc per minute. Our flight time was about thirty minutes so we planned for it all to be in on arrival. I set my watch and gave her 3 cc every three minutes, watched the monitor and spoke to her.

Fifteen minutes later she began deteriorating. I had been retaking her vital signs often and saw the downhill skid coming. I gave the SoluMedrol to Steven to continue and told Eddie I had to take my flight helmet off. While against regulations, he understood and told me over the radio to do what I had to do. I leaned over Teresa and saw her oxygen saturation (sats) falling. We had put on two tanks of oxygen and I was trying to make it last, but now there was no choice. With the first tank almost empty, I switched to the second tank and put Teresa on a non-rebreather mask at 15 liters per minute, rather than the six liters she had been on with the nasal cannula. In theory, this would deliver 98% oxygen but that is only if you have something to deliver it to.

Teresa's sats dropped to 79% and she became more anxious and short of breath. We were trying to beat the clock. Her chest and skin over her abdomen became tighter and I watched as JVDs formed on her neck. I looked through the cervical collar for a tracheal shift, but there was none yet. I told Teresa I thought she might be tensioning and that I might have to needle her. She said, "Yes, I know."

She became more vocal about not being able to catch her breath as I watched her sats plummet to 62%. I got out my 14-gauge needle and prepared the right side of her chest wall for the needle thoracostomy with betadyne swabs. Despite her sats and difficulty breathing, she was still conscious and with the program, and I was determined to needle her only when she developed an altered level or loss of consciousness. I looked out the window and much to my surprise saw the top of the buildings of FMC. I threw on my helmet and kept the needle poised as Steven put in the last of the SoluMedrol. When we landed, Eddie shut down the engines and the ER staff came out with the gurney. I explained the situation and Wyatt, the RN, asked if Teresa could hold out for a chest tube. I said as long as she was talking to me I thought she could. We off-loaded her onto the gurney and off of the roof of the hospital to the elevator. She stayed "with it" the whole time, until we came to the ER. I didn't have to needle her. The new ER had been open only a short time, but it was roomier than the former and allowed more people around the patient. I gave my report as the FMC trauma team took over her care. In a short time, her chest tube was in and the first set of x-rays returned. Ribs were broken everywhere, but the most graphic view was of her lumbar or lower spine. There, the normally aligned individual vertebrae were not even close to each other. Her spinal cord had been totally transected, ripped apart. I knew then she would never walk again. But, she had her arms and her hands, if she lived. She could still be a surgeon, if she lived.

We resupplied as best we could and made our way back to the helicopter on the roof. After we cleaned up we boarded 210 for the flight back to the park. The sun was getting ready to set and the colors were spectacular. I thought briefly of how in a single moment, a life can change so dramatically and permanently. I felt drained but energized all at the same time, and looked down as I wiggled my toes in my leather flight boots. I could not see them but felt them move back and forth, and felt so very lucky.

Epilogue

Teresa was stabilized and transported that evening to Barrow's Neurological Institute in southern Arizona. Her chest injuries began to heal and she was transferred to her hometown for rehabilitation as a paraplegic.

Sitting on my desk is an eight-inch-long piece of black strap. Stiff with dirt but still strong, it is from the life vest that covered Teresa's chest while she waited for rescue on the desert trail. I wonder if I should keep it or send it to her someday.

1450 (Fourteen Fifty)

I was not there . . . Joe was. Rangers, like all people, can get frustrated, angry, and really mad at coworkers. But by the nature of our job, we can forget all of that and instantly rally to the aid of a fellow ranger. Ours is a dangerous job and we need each other to function and to survive. We are, in essence, one big family. I was not there, but I felt like it.

The Blue Ridge Parkway is a beautiful section of National Park scenic drive adjacent to Great Smoky Mountains National Park in North Carolina. It is next to Tennessee and runs through the Cherokee Nation Indian Reservation. It is at the end of a heavily used area, and rangers assigned to cover that area are fewer than those in the heart of the Parkway. As a consequence, when rangers are needed for incidents that occur there, it is often the Smoky Rangers who get there first. Joe was a Smoky Ranger. Tony was assigned to the Blue Ridge, but was forty-five minutes from the end of the drive; Joe less than twenty.

It was June 21 . . . Father's Day. Joe lived fifteen miles outside of the Park and his shift began at 2:30 in the afternoon. We call that "1430" (fourteen-thirty) in military time. He had gone to church then taken his six-year-old daughter and nine-month-old twins, a boy and a girl, to church and to *McDonald's* and then to the baby sitter. His wife, Florie, had already gone to work in the visitor center as an interpreter. His eldest daughter couldn't understand why he had to work on Father's Day. Didn't all dads get Father's Day off? It was a concept she could not yet grasp. Joe told her he had always worked Father's Day, but would try to get it off next year. Joe was diligent, meticulous, and competent. He had put himself through Advanced Life Support School and was an I-EMT, volunteering with the Cherokee Ambulance Crews. He was a complete ranger.

He arrived at work early, about 1410, and was driving to the compound to get his marked patrol car when Ranger Keith drove up. Keith was just coming off shift when a peculiar report came in about a disturbance at Big Witch Gap on the Parkway. Joe told Keith to go on home, that he would take the call. Joe left the compound and headed onto the Parkway. Keith started to leave, then, when he heard more about the call, decided to respond about five minutes later. Ranger Al, too, had received a call and he was less than a mile behind Joe. Tony was at the Ranger Station on the Parkway and had received a report from Dispatch by phone about a man without a shirt, in blue jeans, walking down the middle of the road with a rifle. Tony knew he had a forty-minute estimated time of arrival (ETA) and asked if any Smoky Rangers could respond. They were already en route because several visitors had witnessed this man with the rifle and had reported it.

Reports of people with guns in the Parkway were not at all unusual. After all, it was surrounded by reservation land where it was common to have a firearm and legal to hunt. It was considered normal for any local inhabitant to have a gun in their car, even though it was not legal to have it in Park areas. What was unusual was that a man was walking down the road with it in plain sight.

That man was Jeremiah. He lived on the reservation near Big Cove, had a job, a wife and many children from ages six to nineteen. He was known locally as an excellent woodsman and tracker/hunter. He could move through the wilderness with the ease of a city man walking on a sidewalk. He had hunted all of his life. Jeremiah had a $1,500 Martin guitar and could play it beautifully. But his life was not perfect. His wife, ten years younger at thirty-seven, was estranged. And Jeremiah drank.

Jeremiah woke up early that Father's Day as his wife came home and went to her bed. He put a twelve-pack of beer, his rifle, shotgun, pistol, ammunition and guitar into his beat-up station wagon, and headed onto the dirt roads of the reservation he had known all of his life. He began to drink. It was a rainy morning and the old logging roads were muddy and visibility poor with the fog banks that lingered. By the afternoon, it had begun to clear up and Jeremiah had found himself near a dead end. Suddenly, one front wheel dropped off the rutted road and Jeremiah was stuck. He could not get out. He stashed the shotgun and his beloved guitar in the woods, grabbed his rifle and began to walk out. By just after 2:00 p.m., or 1400, he found himself on the Blue Ridge Parkway near Big Witch Gap.

A Bookstore Association employee drove over the Gap and saw Jeremiah in the road. As she approached him, she saw him shoulder the rifle and point the muzzle right at her through her windshield. She carefully drove around him as he pointed the rifle at her the whole time, pivoting as she drove by. She later said she thought that he would pull the trigger. He didn't. It was a bit of a drive to a phone but she called it in. Now the call had changed from a man with a rifle to a man pointing a rifle at people. This stepped up the response. Layman and Glenn and Helen and Joel were Smoky Rangers who started to roll toward the Gap from the west. Cherokee Nation Police also came from the east.

In the meantime, Jeremiah had walked to the picnic area and asked two teenagers for "chaw" or "ciggas." They did not know what he wanted and were frightened by the rifle. They returned to their car where their parents waited. Jeremiah walked up to the car and stuck the muzzle of the rifle into the chest of the dad, and again asked for "chaw." The dad pushed the barrel away from his chest, said he did not have cigarettes or chewing tobacco, but offered Jeremiah apples and other food. Jeremiah walked away and the family drove off.

It was after 1430 when Joe arrived at the Gap. He called in that he did not see anyone. He drove past the overlook area and rounded a curve past an old road intersection. He saw Jeremiah with the rifle walking down the side of the road and called it in. He drove past him and around another curve where he could safely turn around. On his return, he saw Jeremiah run off into the dense woods with thick understory. Joe stopped just short of an overpass that spanned an old road adjacent to the woods where Jeremiah disappeared. Joe asked Al and Keith to stop on the other side of the west curve, about fifty yards away and try to set up a roadblock to stop oncoming traffic. Joe would do the same on his side. Close the road, turn traffic around, and proceed more directly with the threat when more backup arrived.

Joe was busy. He was coordinating the arriving units on the radio, turning traffic around that came up behind his patrol car with the emergency lights on, and scanning the woods for the man with the gun. He walked in front of his car to the overpass and looked up and down the dirt road below him. At 1446, he called some routine information in to Dispatch, paused then said, "Oh boy." Joe rarely swore. He followed up the exclamation with a report that he could see the man walking down the old dirt road below him from the north, and that he still had the rifle with him. Joe retreated to his patrol car and stood in the "V" of his open driver's door and the car. He continued to coordinate responding units, turn cars around and watch for "the man."

At 1450, Tony arrived and pulled up right behind Joe's patrol car. A van pulled up behind Tony and was instructed to get out of the area. The driver put the van in reverse and started to back away. Tony got out of his patrol car and simultaneously reached for his shotgun. His eyes met Joe's as Joe turned around to acknowledge his arrival. Joe turned back around, and did not see Jeremiah at the top of the overpass on the edge of the Parkway hidden in the woods.

BOOM !!

Those there said the sound of the rifle shot was like a cannon, echoing through the hills and forest. The bullet passed into the left side of Joe's chest, one inch to the left of his National Park Service gold ranger badge in front of his armpit, cutting through the edge of his body armor. Tony watched as Joe stood for a second . . . looked down . . . crumpled to his knees and fell back onto the pavement.

"Shots fired, Officer down, Officer down," came from Tony's radio.

Tony saw the suspect . . . pointed his shotgun and pulled the trigger just as Jeremiah dove out of the way. Pellets slammed into the tree exactly in the spot Jeremiah had been standing. Jeremiah was gone.

BOOM !!

The rear right window of Tony's car had been shot out.

BOOM !!

Another shot, right into the passenger compartment of Joe's vehicle through the windshield and into the headrest. If Joe had dove into the car, it would have been a headshot. Tony moved to the rear bumper of his patrol car trying to locate the shooter.

BOOM!!

Then more shots . . . this time a different caliber . . . smaller, maybe from a pistol. It was impossible to know where they were coming from. Was it the man with the rifle or was it an accomplice? Tony knew he was a sitting duck, continued to wave tourists back and put his car in reverse, moving back down the road about fifty feet.

The van backed down the hill and called in to 911 that they had seen a ranger shot on the Parkway and asked what the hell was going on. You could hear the nine-year-old boy yelling in the background on the 911 tape, "He shot the Ranger, he shot the Ranger!"

Just before the shooting, Al had coordinated with Joe to come back him up with a long rifle. Most law enforcement rangers are issued M16 rifles and are trained in their use along with their other defensive weapons. Joe did not have time to get his rifle when the call came in, so Al was moving up the grassy side of the road on the curve when the first rifle shot exploded. Al could not see Joe and bailed out down into a twenty-foot ravine. He retreated to his car where he could see Joe's car, but could not see Joe.

A Cherokee Police Officer, Julius, arrived behind Tony after Tony had backed up.

BOOM !!

The rifle, again. Julius thought he could hear the ricochet striking the pavement near him. Trackers would later find that Jeremiah had walked, not run, calmly along a dirt road that paralleled the Parkway thirty yards above where Tony and Julius had stopped, and began to fire down on them.

BOOM !!
BOOM !!
BOOM !!

Tony and Julius were pinned down. They radioed in that information and that they couldn't tell the shooter's position.

On the west end, Glenn and Layman arrived. They cleared the picnic area of visitors and ordered up an ambulance and helicopter when they heard the "Officer down" call. They pulled up behind Al, who was hunkered down. They asked who was shot and Al told them it was Joe. The rifle shots resonated through the hills, buzzing their cars. It was impossible to tell where they were coming from or going to. Glenn said they had to go get Joe, but Al told them it would be suicide. Layman was the best shot and Glenn had given him his shotgun and all of his ammunition earlier. There was no plan. There was no panic. There was just the passage of minutes and the repeated methodical sound of the rifle slamming through each one of them.

Tony and Julius counted about ten shots, then a long pause. They took advantage of this to get back into their cars and back down the road another hundred feet or so. Trackers later found the shooter's footprints. Again, they showed a calm walking stride along the parallel dirt road as the shooter pursued Tony. A chill went through Tony as he began to hear a chant. A Cherokee chant . . . a long, moaning, crying, yelling sound directed down toward him. Tony got on the radio that the shooter was hollering down at him and that they should get Joe now . . . but hurry, he could hear him moving back down the road.

Indeed, Jeremiah had broken into a run back down the road, back down toward Joe.

Glenn and Layman and Al and Keith reacted immediately to Tony's call. They drove up in two patrol cars and a pickup truck. Glenn was surprised at how very close they had been to Joe this whole time. They accelerated around the curve and there he was, lying on the ground in a pool of blood. They all stopped short, Layman jumping out with his shotgun, scanning, ready, providing cover. They literally grabbed Joe and threw him into the pickup truck. No one jumped in with him. They needed to get Joe's car out. They did not want to leave a means of escape for the shooter. As they backed out, they had to turn around. Each one knew that the next bullet would hit them. They knew it, felt it. Glenn said it was the longest "K" turn of his life.

They zoomed down the road and in a mile or so met the ambulance. The ambulance crew that responded that day were people Joe worked with often when he worked with the Cherokee ambulance squad. They screeched to a halt and jumped into the pickup with Joe. There was blood everywhere. There was no pulse . . . there was no breathing. Glenn pulled Joe's uniform shirt open, ripping away the buttons. He handed Joe's gun to Helen to secure it. It had not been fired. There is little defense against an ambush. Joel was cutting at his shirt and pulling off his body armor. They started compressions. Glenn did mouth-to-mouth through the blood until a mask and bag were brought. They intubated him, placing a tube down his throat to put air into the trachea and into his lungs. They started intravenous lines. They saw the bullet hole through his left shoulder and wondered how such a wound could do this. As they prepared to put him in the ambulance, they turned him over.

The exit wound on the back of his right shoulder was enormous; almost as big as the palm of a hand. The rifle shot was equivalent to a .308. Traveling at more than two thousand feet per second, it compressed the air in front of it, creating a dense concussive wave. When it slammed into Joe, the bullet may have been only a third of an inch in diameter, but it had the destructive diameter the size of a baseball, traveling beyond the speed of sound. It took out Joe's left lung, obliterated his windpipe, transected his aorta and blew an exit hole in his right scapula (shoulder blade). By the time Joe looked down and before he collapsed, the bullet was a half-mile down the road. Objectively, it was a remarkable shot. Jeremiah did not have a scope on his rifle, just a pop-up site. Many speculate Jeremiah was aiming for Joe's ranger badge. He was an excellent shot. It did the most destruction possible, and killed Joe almost instantly.

They raced down to the helicopter landing site. They knew Joe was dead, but they couldn't stop trying. The landing zone was not clear so they called and asked the interpreter on duty to clear the parking lot of the visitor center for the helicopter. Florie, Joe's wife, ran out to clear the way.

The ambulance arrived and the Flight Paramedic jumped in. They defibrillated Joe and started a round of heart drugs. The medic knew Joe. They carried him out of the ambulance to the helicopter. Florie gave Joe's feet a quick squeeze and told him she loved him. Glenn would not leave him alone and jumped into the helicopter with Joe.

When they arrived at the Trauma Center in Knoxville, it was just a matter of minutes before they declared Joe dead.

In the meantime, the manhunt was on.

Over one hundred officers from all jurisdictions and agencies descended on the Parkway. Two Cherokee Fish and Game Officers called in to a local police department to volunteer and were told to wait for instructions. One of the officers, Dave, who grew up in the area and knew the country, said to his partner he believed whoever did this knew the country, too, and would most probably go down the drainage below the Gap. Dave drove into the maze of dirt roads to an abandoned cabin at the end of the drainage and sat on a picnic table and waited.

Four SWAT teams arrived, scores of officers, helicopters, and crime scene specialists. The FBI was on its way. In the meantime, Jeremiah had left his rifle on the mountain. He apparently did not have it when he chanted or when he ran back down the road. Perhaps when he went to pick it up he could not find it. He kept going, down an old logging road below the Gap. He headed for the creek, took the remaining rifle rounds out of his pocket and set them on the embankment, then jumped. He walked downstream through the creek. As he came out onto an old dirt road near an abandoned cabin, he saw Dave. They knew each other. They grew up together.

Dave said, "Hey Jeremiah, did you have anything to do with that shooting up there?"

Jeremiah said no, that he only had a shotgun and it was back at his car stuck on a road and he was walking home. Jeremiah began to walk past Dave, who was a big bear of a man. Dave told him to stop. Jeremiah did. Dave called for his partner, who came over. Jeremiah was read his Miranda Rights by the two Fish and Game Officers. Jeremiah said he wanted a lawyer. Dave called the Incident Commander and said, "Hey, I think we got your guy over here."

While waiting for the other officers, Dave's partner asked if he had anything to do with the shooting Jeremiah said, "No, I only had my shotgun, that guy was shot with a rifle." Bingo. They had him. Except that admission was never to be used in court. Once a suspect in custody has invoked his Miranda Rights, in this case requesting a lawyer, no one can ask him questions about the crime without his lawyer being present. Because further questioning violated his rights, that admission of obvious knowledge about the shooting was inadmissible. As it turned out, they wouldn't need it.

All of the evidence pointed directly to Jeremiah. The defense never argued that he didn't do it. The fight was for his life. They argued that he was drunk and had amnesia and there was no premeditation. They wanted murder in the second degree. The prosecution wanted murder in the first degree, which involved either premeditation or laying-in-wait . . . ambushing someone. At first the jury thought it had to be both premeditation and laying and were deadlocked. Once they realized, after clarification, they only needed one or the other, they found Jeremiah guilty of first-degree murder with a sentence of a natural lifetime in jail . . . in short, incarceration until he died.

Most of the rangers involved have moved to other Parks. A presentation of the events is being offered at other Parks so rangers can learn from the events. We had that presentation at Grand Canyon and it was wrenching. One of the rangers involved, Glenn, transferred to Grand Canyon and worked with me on the South Rim. I first met Glenn in Florida when we were both on the Hurricane Andrew Response Team. I have a group picture of us from that event and showed it to Glenn. There we were, about fifteen of us ready to battle the crowds that were accumulating for the Columbus Day Regatta.

Glenn said, "Remember that naked lady we treated for a drug overdose?"

I said, "Do I ever? I started that IV in a speed boat going 30 knots."

Glenn said, "It's still the best IV start I have ever seen. Do you remember who helped us on that call?"

I said, "I think so."

Glenn took the picture from my hands and pointed to the bearded ranger to my right.

"Sure, I remember Joe ...." Then it hit me; this was the Joe who had been murdered in the Smokys. Our lives had touched briefly during a twenty-one day detail to Florida after Hurricane Andrew. We were on the Resource Team assigned to help persons left injured and homeless after the devastation. I had known this quiet capable man only briefly, and now he was gone. I was stunned. I felt very, very mortal and humbled. The realities of this life are sometimes too close to home. I took the photo back home and put it back on the wall where it hung attached to a red and black square hurricane flag. The flag and photo have a whole new meaning to me now.

The Elk

■ Grand Canyon, Arizona

Karyn is one of my very good friends. She also happens to be the very best dispatcher I have ever worked with. She is quick and efficient, anticipates needs and, above all, is very professional. Never in her tone of voice will you hear her be snide or short or worried. Karyn knows her number one job is to be there for me, to be my number one backup.

There is a wonderful little clipping I have taped to my desk in the Ranger Operations Building. It says:

> *You may know where you are,*
> *and God may know where you are,*
> *but unless your Dispatcher knows where you are,*
> *you'd better be on good terms with your God.*

In order for Dispatch to provide us help as needed, we must give them specific information. If we stop a vehicle, we radio to Dispatch the place of the stop, the license plate number, a brief description of the car and the number of occupants. If they ask for a status check and we don't respond with a preset coded answer, they will alert other Protection Rangers who will respond immediately. Woe be it to the ranger who gives the wrong code and then gets mad at the Dispatcher for sending backup. That is truly cutting their safety line! But it happens. Everything happens.

That is why we train and train, and train some more. We practice handcuffing, defensive tactics, and shooting situations at the range. I learned early on that in order to hit the target at the range I had to pretty much ignore the target. If it was in focus, I wasn't aiming right. The key was to line up the front sight of the pistol between and even with the two back sights. With these three aligned and in focus, the target was recognizable in the distance but was an out-of-focus blur. By aiming toward center mass, I couldn't miss. Slow, steady trigger pull and trying not to anticipate the discharge of the gun are all key to hitting the target center mass. With practice, it becomes second nature and you develop muscle memory. I got so good that I shot 294 out of 300 at the Federal Law Enforcement Training Center during academy qualifications.

That night I was on the night shift with co-worker Kent. Amazingly, of the four men named Kent I have ever met, they have all been Park Rangers. Since there were three Kents in Grand Canyon, I often referred to my husband as "my Kent." This other Kent was married to Paramedic Tammy. Winter night shifts can be cold and quiet or cold and busy. This was to be a busy one and it would result in me making a jail run. To put it simply, I would make an arrest and then transport the prisoner eighty miles, or one-and-a-half hours to Flagstaff from Grand Canyon National Park. This would be done at night, on rural highways without streetlights, with wildlife everywhere, including elk that can weigh close to one thousand pounds. I hated winter nighttime jail runs. It demanded the hyper-alertness necessary to keep from hitting an elk, deer, coyote or other creature that decided it just had to run out in front of my car; the driving savvy to hit black ice and not hit the brakes while steering with the spin; the stamina to drive three hours on dark lonely roads with the fortitude to not fall asleep at the wheel, though I had been up forever doing my job because we had been so shorthanded; and the patience to treat arrestees like human beings even though they may have tried to bite, spit, or just plain vomit on me.

I often did jail runs with my window down and outside air temperature of six degrees Fahrenheit, as the smell of the intoxicated prisoner in the back seat behind the cage was overwhelming. They may have defecated in their pants, vomited on themselves, or had such a high blood alcohol level that it smelled like a brewery … or all mixed in together. (And people wonder why I can't stand the smell of alcoholic beverages). A glamour job this was not. Therefore, using the phrase, "watch for elk" meant more than just watching out for wildlife. It meant be careful, be alert, be safe, and come back alive and in one piece.

By early evening we had responded to several calls. Karyn was at Dispatch sending us to different situations. Depending on the call we would respond singly or en masse. Just in case a ranger may not get the clue from the dispatcher that a call is serious, a series of alert tones are used to grab attention and keep others off the air while the call is given to the case ranger. A "high low" alert tone is for emergencies, including medical emergencies and structural fires, plane crashes and falls from the rim. A broken, monotone alert is for law enforcement incidents. This includes a fight in progress, robbery, alarm, burglary or other situation requiring immediate law enforcement response. One long and steady tone is an alert to pay attention. Dispatch then broadcasts what we call "BOLs" (be on the lookout for ...) as well as any other information of a non-emergent but urgent concern. There is no ranger on the job at Grand Canyon that does not get a bit of an adrenaline rush when they hear an alert tone. That is a call to action, something out of the ordinary, something life threatening or something of great importance. It is about to be broadcast, and it is that ranger's job to deal with it. No matter what happens, when you are a Protection Ranger, you have to deal with it.

A bit of anxiety is good. It makes you more alert and focused to do your job. Moderate to severe anxiety can inhibit a person to the point where they get tunnel vision or can only do one thing at a time. You can tell the long-term rangers from the new ones. Experienced rangers pride themselves on using a very calm but determined voice on the radio in a crisis; walking not running to their patrol vehicle; and putting their seat belt on before the first turn in the road. New rangers are so hyped sometimes you can hear their voices go up two octaves on the radio, and you feel like giving them Valium and picking them up after the call. But without the experience and participation, they will never learn. So tolerance and a smirk is the order of the day. After all, we were all new, once.

At 7:10 p.m., Karyn sounded the beeping monotone alert tone that immediately signaled a serious law enforcement incident. The call was to respond to Rouzer Hall for a domestic fight in progress ... unknown if weapons were involved. More law enforcement officers are hurt and killed during domestic violence calls than any other. These calls are volatile, full of anger and emotion, and always involve more than one person. It is not uncommon for an officer to arrest one spouse for hitting the other, and the moment the spouse is handcuffed, the victim attacks the officer for taking their loved one to jail! There is little rationality to these calls. And almost all of them involve alcohol. This one did also.

Rouzer Hall is a dormitory of mixed gender, housing the employees of the concessionaire. The concessionaire are the people who contract with the National Park Service to run the various facilities in the park, such as gas stations, hotels and gift stores. They also provide a variety of services to the general public, such as mule rides and bus tours. Not many people want to live far from any city and receive minimum wage for cleaning bathrooms, bussing tables or making beds. Many, not all, of the employees have had problems in their past life, have little education or job skills, and have little motivation to do constructive things with their off work time. Many, many, many, turn to drugs and alcohol ... the latter being the poison of choice. By far, the majority of law enforcement calls involve intoxicated persons.

When we arrived at Rouzer Hall I headed into the parking lot while Ranger Kent parked on the backside. We entered the building through different doors and could hear the yelling and pounding and cursing. We approached Room 10 and saw a 24-year-old female on the hallway floor being pinned to the ground by two other females. The "pinnee" was Michelle, also known as "Billie." Billie was being held by "pinners," Cindy and Lisa. Billie, who was yelling and spitting and kicking and flailing, was 5'5" tall and over 170 pounds. She had bloody knuckles and was swearing like a sea captain. Kent and I made sure we had gloves on before we relieved Cindy and Lisa. As we took over and tried to calm Billie to release our hold on her, she became even more violent, trying to bite us and spit on us. I held her in an arm lock and pressed her torso to the carpet with my knee in the middle of her shoulders. There was the distinctive odor of an alcoholic beverage on her breath and all attempts to calm her were in vain. I placed her in handcuffs, checked them for tightness, set the double lock and rechecked for tightness. This is drilled into you at the academy. It would not be a good thing to even routinely handcuff a suspect and not check and double lock. There have been cases where people have claimed injuries. In one, a neurosurgeon claimed he had nerve damage to his hands and could not operate anymore because this small detail was not completed. That claim cost the offending department millions of dollars in settlement costs.

While I was dealing with the upper body, Kent was seeing to the lower. He held her legs down to keep her from kicking him, and then was able to turn the task over to a Fire and Safety employee ... one of the concession employees who work to keep their buildings and guests safe, and who are of great assistance to us. They are not commissioned law enforcement officers, but play an important peripheral role.

Kent and I learned that the victim was in Room 10. I turned my charge over to Kent and interviewed the victim, Billie's mother, Florine. At fifty-one years of age, Florine looked eighty, and that did not include the recent bloodied lip and bruising on her face and arms. Florine was pretty noncommittal, saying, "Billie gets this way sometimes when she drinks," adding, "but she doesn't always hit me." Florine declined transport to the clinic and our attention was turned back to Billie.

The law can be pretty frustrating. A misdemeanor is not one

of the big common law crimes. Common law crimes are felonies and include murder, burglary, robbery, aggravated assault and rape. In a felony, an arrest can occur as a result of an officer's investigation, even if the officer did not see the crime being committed. Misdemeanor laws under the current federal system include traffic violations, thefts less than $1,000, fights, and disorderly conduct. For the most part, an officer is not allowed to arrest anyone for a misdemeanor not created in his or her presence. And even if the misdemeanor was created in their presence, a violator is not usually arrested. You give them a ticket (to pay a fine or appear in court) or a warning (written or verbal). Sometimes you really know when someone needs to be arrested, to be taken out of the community for a while. This was one of those times. The trouble was, we did not see Billie hit her mom, and simple assault is a misdemeanor. But we did see other things.

Billie was violating two misdemeanors in our presence. It's not illegal to be drunk in public. But if you are so intoxicated that you damage property, hurt someone or put yourself in danger (say, by walking home by following the yellow line in the middle of the roadway), then that is a violation. Billie was also kind enough to breach the public peace by her disorderly conduct. Using swear words where the public can hear them and become offended by them is a violation. (By law, a law enforcement officer cannot be offended by swear words). In addition, she was resisting arrest, so we quickly decided she was a "10-15." (The 10 code is rarely used, but we use it at times as radio slang. 10-15 is code for saying someone is in custody . . . under arrest).

Billie was a sight to behold by this time. She was so violent; we placed a web band around her ankles to keep her from kicking us. She was swearing, spitting, trying to buck and roll. She was an Olympic contender, let me tell you. Where do drunks get all of that energy? They are truly in another world. It took four of us to physically carry her to my patrol car. We picked her up by each shoulder and arm, hips and legs, ever mindful of teeth, spit and kicks. We placed her down on the back seat of my patrol car, and I slipped the tail of the webbing through the back door and closed it to catch my breath. Before I even got in one inhalation, she had pulled the strap loose and was on her back, kicking mightily at the window, almost breaking it. I quickly opened the door, pulled the strap back through with a knot in it and closed the door above the knot. Now she could not kick out the window. Kent and I worked her into a seat belt and finally drove the three miles to the small Jail Booking facility we have.

Once a prisoner is booked, they are either transported to Coconino County Jail in Flagstaff, eighty miles away, or released on cash bail bond or on their own recognizance. Billie did not meet our release criteria and was going south. Once that reality hit her, she became a changed woman. She stopped swearing and fighting, and we were able to photograph and fingerprint her. She even consented to an alcohol breath test and blew a whopping 0.264 alcohol content. Most people know that drunk driving is a 0.08 alcohol content ... and Billie was over three times that! Amazing. Some alcoholics need booze so much that they don't even become functional until they are over 0.10 ... very sad. But this was tragic. She was too young to be in this downward spiral.

By 8:45 p.m. I was ready to do the transport. I had a new Caprice that drove well, had a good heater and a smooth ride. But Kent said I needed to take "the clunker." They needed to build up miles on it so they could turn it in for a new car. It was an older model Chevrolet sedan with a lot of hard miles, currently assigned to the District Ranger. It had that very used car smell, rattled when you exceeded 50 mph, and had a "waffle," an open steel cage between the prisoner and the driver/officer instead of an acrylic window. That meant that spit could reach the back of my neck. I was not looking forward to this and was more than sweet to Billie so she wouldn't return to her evil ways on the way to town.

Billie was placed in the back seat with her transport belt on. This allowed her hands to be cuffed in front of her waist, which is more comfortable. I put on her seat belt and she leaned her head against the window and began to doze. I began to think this could be my lucky night. I quietly got in, called to Dispatch that I was en route with the prisoner to Flagstaff, and began the drive south.

The Grand Canyon is on a plateau, a high rim at 7,000 feet in elevation. The road south is almost straight for twenty-eight miles to a small intersection called Valle. There, the road splits and continues south to Williams on Hwy 64, where you can pick up Interstate 40 to Flagstaff. You can also go east at Valle, taking Hwy 180 through some hills and up above 8,000 feet into Flagstaff. I try to avoid Hwy 180 at night because it is harder to see wildlife for the many pine trees and reaction time is less. It also accumulates more snow and ice. I let my dispatch know I was going the Williams route.

We drove quietly through the mixed pine just south of the canyon. The road became very straight as we broke through the tree line and headed on a slight downhill slope toward Valle. It was about 9:15 p.m. when I could see two sets of headlights off in the distance. The cars were about two miles south and I watched as I anticipated the headlights in my lane of traffic to merge back into the northbound lane after passing the other vehicle. As the seconds ticked by, I watched the one set of headlights stay in my lane. I sat up straighter and realized that something was wrong.

The hair on the back of my neck began to tingle, and I picked up my radio microphone. I was now about twenty miles south of the Park. I called out to Dispatch my location, "about mile marker 220." I was relieved to hear Karyn answer that she was able to hear me, even though her transmission was weak and scratchy. I added, "I don't know what's going on but I have two vehicles coming my way, and one is in my lane ... I may have a drunk driver." When it became apparent that the vehicle in my lane was not going to move, I reached over and turned on my overhead rotating lights on my patrol car light bar and keyed on my high beams and spotlight. Everybody began to slow down. I stayed in my lane with my lights on as a full-size yellow Dodge Ramcharger truck pulled to within sixty-five feet of the front of my patrol car and came to a stop.

From my position in my sedan, I had to look up at the driver in the truck who was now clearly illuminated in my high beams and spotlights. The driver was an approximately 55-year-old male. He sat behind the wheel, with a dazed, almost blank look on his face. I put my car into park and looked over at the second vehicle in the northbound lane as it came to a stop side by side with the truck. It was a small blue Toyota pickup truck with several people in the cab. The front end of the Toyota was badly damaged. It was apparent the folks in the Toyota were yelling to me and their words became clearer as I opened my car door. I stood up by putting my left foot on the pavement. I distinctly heard a man yell, "He hit us, he's drunk, he tried to kill us!" I was mesmerized for a very brief moment at the man's Scottish accent, looking toward the sound of the voice. Then the roaring of the Ramcharger's gunning engine and the sound of it being put into gear set me into instant motion.

With no time to get back in the vehicle, I crouched down, put the column shifter into reverse and slammed on the accelerator. With my driver's door open and my left leg dangling above the pavement, I surged backward in my lane, looking up as the towering Ramcharger came bearing down on me. The huge truck had barely missed slamming into me and crushing me under my own vehicle. I steered and reached for the microphone at the same time. I had covered one hundred feet backwards with the Ramcharger still in pursuit, still with my door open and my leg out when, from seemingly out of nowhere, the crunched little Toyota accelerated past the Ramcharger, and cut in front of it, placing themselves between myself and the oncoming menace. This forced the Ramcharger off at an angle and it came to a halt, the engine stalling then stopping. I keyed the microphone as I came to a stop and called in to Dispatch: "Dispatch, there's been an accident. Someone tried to run me over; it's Arizona plate DE--95, a yellow Dodge truck. I need backup ... send somebody, anybody!"

I did fine until the last line ... I'm sure my voice went up half an octave and, believe me, I sounded urgent. So much for a calm, professional, experienced demeanor when someone is trying to kill you.

I ended up about thirty feet from the Ramcharger and with my door still open, called to the folks in the Toyota to back down the road and wait out of the way. They instantly complied. As I stood in the "V" between my open driver door and the vehicle, I heard a faint voice come from inside my car. As I watched the Ramcharger driver intently for his next move, I could hear my prisoner, Billie say, "He tried to hit us." Boy, she had sobered up in a hurry.

I called out to the driver of the Ramcharger and identified myself as a police officer. I then ordered the driver to get out of his truck. He did not comply. Instead he leaned forward and appeared to be trying to reach for something on the floor by his feet. That was it. I couldn't see his hands and that's a bad thing. For all I knew, he could be reaching for a gun! I pulled my 9 mm semiautomatic pistol from its holster, and pointed it at the driver. While staying in the protective "V" of my car (we are trained to believe that engine blocks can stop bullets better than car doors), I ordered the driver out again. This time, he sat up, and I distinctly heard him through his open window yell back: "F--- you!" I ordered him again, with the same response, and again, and again, and again. I gave a total of seven orders to exit his vehicle, and received the same, unoriginal response from the driver. He again tried to reach for something between his legs. I took a deep breath, quite consciously, and ordered him out again.

I could hear indistinct radio traffic in the background but it was the flashing lights of a police car many miles to the south of my position that caught my eye. I hoped my backup would come in time. I again ordered the driver out of the truck and, much to my surprise, he opened his door and began to get out. My eyes strained to see his hands, and what might be in them. He tripped over something in the doorway, got out of the truck and slammed his door closed. His hands were empty. I stood a little straighter, and lowered my gun.

I ordered the driver to lay face down on the ground. This time, he was a little more creative. He yelled back to me, "No, suck my d---!" I ordered him down three more times in the same, loud, authoritative voice, and received equally colorful metaphors back. (Use your imagination. If you thought of it, he said it).

He walked in a little circle by his front left headlight and, much to my relief, finally lay face down on the ground in a push-up position. I then ordered him to turn his face away from me and put his hands out to the side with his palms up. (Once a suspect does this and crosses his ankles, you can then approach them without them seeing you and handcuff them ... hopefully after your backup arrives). Unfortunately, the driver refused, yelled more expletives and rose up onto his elbows. I ordered him back down. Again he refused and then stood up. It was then that I noted the leather holster on his belt.

It was partially concealed by a shirttail. I immediately told the driver that I saw the holster and that he was to keep his hands away from it. I asked him if it was a knife or a gun. He said it was a knife and began to reach for the holster. I ordered him to stop and take his hand away from the holster. I still couldn't tell if it was a gun or a knife holster. If it was a gun, I was threatened at any range. If it was a knife, that could be different. We are trained to not perceive knives as an immediate threat, as long as the suspect is more than twenty-one feet away. Twenty-one feet is the magic number. Studies have shown that a suspect can pull a knife, lunge and stab an officer before the officer, with their gun drawn, can react.

There are many, many cases on the books of an officer-involved shooting involving a suspect with a knife. If the knife-wielding suspect is twenty-one feet or closer, the shooting is deemed justified. If farther, the courts are hard pressed to justify the shooting, stating the officer had time and distance and was not in immediate danger. No one wants to shoot another, but no one wants to get stabbed either. A lot of officers can visually mark out a twenty-one foot distance out of practice, so if they are put in a bad position, they protect themselves and don't have to face charges in a "bad shooting."

The driver was thirty feet away and I knew I was still okay if it was a knife, but a gun would be different. I crouched lower in my "V" and ordered the driver down again. I raised my gun from its low ready position (pointing toward the ground at a 45-degree angle) and pointed it at the driver/suspect. Again the driver refused to take his hand off the holster and began to fumble with it, walking in front of his truck, toward me. I ordered him to stop, calling out "Police, stop!" but still he came toward me with his hand on the holster. He was easily within twenty feet of me and my training took over.

The suspect began to go out of focus as I lined up the sights on my pistol.

I yelled, "Stop, or I'll shoot," and still he came toward me.

He was now less than fifteen feet away. I knew I was going to shoot him. I knew I had to stop him. I knew, without a doubt, I would kill him.

I began to slowly squeeze the trigger with a perfect sight alignment on his center mass and called out, "Stop, or I'll kill you."

He stopped.

I stopped.

The trigger was weightless under my finger, the fuzzy target began to retreat. He took his hand off the holster. As I released the trigger and brought the driver back into focus, I watched as he returned to the front of his truck and then around to the driver's side. I never moved. I quickly called out to him to lie down, and he got to his knees. To me, it was a miracle.

As he fell to his knees, Coconino County Sheriff Deputy Glenn arrived from the south and parked off the road behind the Toyota. I glanced toward Glenn and saw him remove his side arm and run at a crouch up the road behind the Toyota. In an instant I knew he had no idea what was up, but I had worked with him enough to build up a trust. I called to him, "Suspect, turquoise shirt, driver's side Dodge truck." That was all he needed. He sprinted behind the Dodge, and was on the driver in seconds. With a helping hand to the middle of his back, Glenn shoved the suspect the rest of the way to the pavement from his kneeling position. The driver never saw him coming.

I came from around my door and trained my pistol on the driver. I mentioned the holster to Glenn as he holstered his own weapon and handcuffed the suspect. I put my gun away and snapped the retaining piece methodically. I breathed. I helped Glenn to restrain the driver while we searched him. We removed a five-inch-long hunting knife from the leather holster on his belt. I stayed with the driver, pinning him to the ground, while Glenn went back to get his patrol truck. Because I already had a prisoner, Glenn would have to put the suspect in the front of his pickup truck.

The driver had the odor of an alcoholic beverage on his breath and appeared intoxicated. (He would, hours later, still record more than twice the legal limit of alcohol intoxication for DUI). It was a cold fifth of October and we couldn't leave him on the pavement. So we hauled him up and put him in the passenger side of Glenn's patrol truck with the seat belt on, and closed the door. We had his wallet from the search of his person as a result of the arrest. We found the driver's identification; his name was Arthur. I then headed toward the Toyota to get their story and see if anyone was injured. As I walked by the closed door of the Ramcharger I looked in the driver's window to see what Arthur had been reaching for. There, on the floor of the driver's compartment, was a loaded .357 magnum revolver half out of its holster.

As I walked to the Toyota, I saw the three passengers exit. The driver was Kenneth from Scotland. He said he was okay, and his passengers were okay. I excused myself for a moment and returned to my patrol car. Billie was fine in the back seat, dozing now that all the "fun" was over. I got on the radio and told Dispatch I was "code 4" (okay), and had one in custody with weapons. I added that Coconino County had a Sheriff's Deputy on scene, and I was requesting DPS. DPS is the Department of Public Safety in Arizona, what they call their Highway Patrol. This was their jurisdiction, and ultimately their case and prisoner. I was merely "assisting" them.

Dispatch again confirmed my status and asked if I needed any more officers from the Park on scene. I said no, that the Sheriff's department and DPS would take over. I heard her cancel several responding units from the park. Yeah for Dispatch ... no fewer than three police cars with officers were on their way to back me up. Glenn just happened to be closer, only ten miles away at Valle. I filled in Glenn. He had been on the radio with his own dispatcher. He knew I had a prisoner transport to complete and was requesting another Sheriff Deputy on scene so I could complete my jail run. We knew DPS was shorthanded and would be a while.

When I returned to Kenneth, he told me a story that was so incredible, that if I didn't have the evidence in front of me, I would have a hard time believing it. Apparently, they had visited the Grand Canyon that day with an American friend's borrowed Toyota pickup truck. They were visiting from Scotland and just loved the southwest. After visiting the canyon, they had driven almost forty miles south on Hwy 64 toward Williams and past Valle. Soon after, Arthur and his pickup truck left his northbound lane and hit them head-on in their little Toyota pickup, spinning them around. They saw that the truck had been smashed, but they were remarkably okay, having worn their seat belts. When they realized the driver of the Dodger Ramcharger was not stopping, indeed, he was continuing north in the southbound lane, they began to chase him.

They knew it was not their truck and not their fault, but who would believe them in America without evidence? As they followed Arthur in his truck north, with their radiator hissing and wheels wobbling, they began to videotape his driving behavior as he swerved from lane to lane, sometimes driving off the highway and running many other cars off of the road. They even took still pictures. I was blown away, knowing now that Arthur had a very powerful gun and could have shot at them at any time.

I asked Kenneth what he planned to do when he caught the driver. Kenneth said he didn't plan to catch the driver. He knew from television that America was full of police officers and that they planned to follow the suspect until an officer showed up. I thought their logic faulty and their impression of America all wrong until I realized that their plan had worked. They had followed him right to me. They stood there with the self-satisfaction of knowing their plan had worked. I told them they needed to stay on scene until the DPS Officer arrived, and again asked if they were okay. They said yes, and that they had a thermos and food and would wait patiently in their bent-up truck. I shook my head and walked back to my car.

There, Billie continued her nap in the still running, heated patrol car. I walked back to Glenn and told him about the events of the evening. He walked over and looked at the pistol on the floor of Arthur's car. We agreed it had been a close call.

Finally, another Deputy arrived, Sergeant Dave. He parked his sedan in front of Glenn's truck, and was filled in. He said he had been in contact with DPS and an officer was about thirty minutes out. He said I would have to return to the crime scene as soon as possible to talk to DPS because I was the arresting officer. I told him I would, and was released from the scene to continue my jail run. To expedite things, I thought I would take a chance and take the quicker way to Flagstaff Jail by going on Hwy 180 out of Valle.

As I began to enter my car to leave, Arthur went ballistic in the cab of the Sheriff Deputy's truck. He kicked and yelled and threw his body back and forth. He managed to pull the microphone cord out of the radio and kick the gearshift into neutral. The deputy's truck rolled forward and smashed into the back of the sergeant's sedan, denting it severely. I knew this was my cue to leave as the two deputies headed for the truck with words that matched Arthur's.

Remarkably, I made it to the jail about an hour later without mishap.

The jail is a complex area that follows very strict rules. When I arrived at the jail off Cherry Street in Flagstaff to approach the prisoner entry area, I stopped at an intercom and stated my identity and business in full view of a video camera. Within a minute a large automatic door rose up, and I drove into the sally port and made sure the door in front of me was closed and waited until the door behind me was also closed. This way, if a suspect ran from the car, they would still be in the sally port instead of running through the streets of downtown Flagstaff at midnight. I proceeded to a lock up area and removed my pistol, ammunition and pepper spray container and put them in a small safe, locked it, and kept the key. No one is allowed in the jail with any weapons – not even the jailers. Should an officer lose a weapon to a prisoner in that environment, the consequences could be frightful. I then removed my prisoner from the car.

At this point, Billie was a new woman. We walked to the first of two locked doors in full view of the jailers who watched us through thick glass windows. The jailers electronically released the outer door and we entered. Like an airlock, they waited for the outer door to close and lock before opening the inner door. During this time, Billie apologized to me. She was really sorry she tried to bite me and kick me and spit on me. She was really sorry she beat up her mother ... again. She was really sorry. The first time she told me I felt better. The fifth round of identical apologies began to grate on me. It had been a long night.

I entered the booking area with Billie and gave the jailers her paperwork and turned Billie over to them. They searched her again, asked her questions about her health and medications she was taking, and if she was suicidal. They removed my transport belt and handcuffs and returned them to me. Billie was led away to her jail cell to sleep it off before her initial appearance before the U.S. Judge Magistrate the next day.

The jailers said they heard some of the radio traffic about my DUI arrest during my prisoner transport. I gave them the short version and told them I needed to get back to fill in the DPS Officer. They offered me coffee for the drive back, but I don't drink coffee. I realized caffeine would be a good idea, so I asked if the *McDonald's* on Milton Avenue was still open. They didn't think so, but one officer was sure the *Jack in the Box* near it would be. I thanked them and left the booking area. I retrieved my defensive equipment, and entered my car and waited for the front door to open. With a clatter it rolled up and out of the way. I waited for it to open completely. I didn't want to leave too soon and knock the light bar off of my vehicle.

As I drove through downtown, it was quiet and calm and the streetlights put out a soft glow. I headed past City Hall and looked up toward Mars Hill where Lowell Observatory resides. As I turned south on Milton Ave., I noted a frenzy of activity ahead and realized there was a siren behind me. I pulled over as a fire department ladder truck raced by with its lights and sirens on. As I pulled out I felt glad I didn't have to respond. Then I saw where the fire was located … at the *Jack in the Box*.

Firefighters were climbing ladders and spraying water onto the roof as smoke billowed from under the eaves. I stopped in the middle of the street thinking I'm jinxed and that I should have taken the day off. No cola tonight, so I headed for the freeway and caught it west to Williams.

As I traveled, I received radio traffic on the county frequency. I was told that DPS was finished on scene and would like to meet me at mile marker 190 on Hwy 64 north of Williams. I acknowledged in the affirmative and continued to the Hwy 64 exit out of Williams. I was anxious to hear what DPS had found. As I headed north on Hwy 64, I realized a lot of the mile markers were missing. I slowed down near my meeting place and at mile marker 195, a huge object going at great speed filled my vision on the left side of my windshield. It was an elk.

It was running across the road. I hit the brakes and instantly knew I would miss it; as long as it kept running, I would miss it. I refused to swerve, for that would make the car roll and keep me from being protected by my engine block. I slid, skidding forward. The elk stopped. I couldn't believe it stopped. I hit it, dead center. It took out the front of my grill, powered into my windshield and smashed toward me. By this time I had stopped moving and my forward momentum shifted to shed the elk from my car. It fell onto the pavement and rolled down the dirt embankment to the trees below.

I sat there, stunned. I couldn't believe this had happened. I had never hit a deer or elk or any large animal in my life. The ignition was still on but the engine was not. I could see the steam escaping from my smashed radiator, rising in my dimming headlights. I had smashed a government car. Oh, the paperwork! I quickly reviewed the events and realized there was nothing I could have done. I had been going ten miles below the speed limit (thank goodness), and it was just one of those things.

I took a deep breath and in my calm, experienced radio voice began, "Dispatch, 523."

"523, Dispatch," she replied.

"I am code 4 at mile marker 192, but I have hit THE ELK."

There was the briefest of pauses at the other end, and then Karyn's voice returned. She knew the night I had, and for the first time, I read some emotion in her voice. It was a combination of frustration and deep compassion for me. She replied:

"Copy 523, you are code 4 at mile marker 192, do you need any assistance?"

I told her I had no injuries but the car was totaled and that I would need a tow truck. I asked her to send the DPS Officer I was to meet to my location and that I would get back to her on the status of the elk. Karyn told me later that when I first called in hitting the elk she thought I was kidding. My voice was so calm and she knew I dreaded jail runs for these very reasons. Now my nightmare had come true, and she knew it.

I turned the ignition off, pulled on my hazard lights and kept my headlights on. I climbed out of my car and the cold air hit me full force. I looked calmly at the front of my vehicle, somewhat detached. I saw the hood bent up almost to the windshield, which was cracked with a bursting star pattern. I looked down at the steaming gnarled radiator remains and the pool of antifreeze accumulating on the pavement. A grunting sound caught my attention and I pulled out my flashlight and went down the embankment. It was a cow (female) elk, later estimated at eight hundred pounds. She was still alive with injuries not compatible with life. She didn't even have the decency to die right away. Now I would have to finish the job.

I looked at her fractured legs, open belly wounds and blood coming from her nose one more time to be sure I was making the correct decision. It's not an easy thing to take a life ... any life. I waited a moment to see if perhaps her breathing was agonal, and she would die shortly. There was no evidence of that. If I did not intervene, chances were she would lie there suffering for hours in the cold, perhaps not even dying before the coyotes found her. I knew I had to put her down.

I pulled out my semiautomatic pistol and pointed a flashlight at her skull above her brain. I prepared my sight alignment, holding my pistol in one hand. As my sights lined up and my target went out of focus, I squeezed the trigger slowly. A large flash of fire and loud blast were released in that dark quiet night. The elk's body jerked one last time, and then she was still. I lowered my gun and trained the light on her skull. The bullet had penetrated just where I wanted. She was gone, quickly and efficiently. I reholstered and walked away from the elk and returned to my car to wait for the DPS Officer.

DPS Officer Jay arrived on scene just after midnight. I had called in my status to Dispatch after putting down the elk, and waited patiently. Jay was affable and remarkably light about my situation. He said he would be happy to do my motor vehicle accident (MVA) report, and thanked me for dispatching the elk so he wouldn't have to. He said this happens so much on these highways. But before he would do my report, Jay beckoned me to his patrol car. He wanted to show me something. He didn't have Arthur with him. He said Sgt. Dave was kind enough to do the transport to jail so Jay could come and talk to me. But he did have the contents of the cab of Arthur's truck with him.

Jay opened the driver door of his patrol sedan and in the dome light I could see an arsenal.

There was the .357 magnum pistol I had seen. There was a shotgun that had been loaded, sitting at an angle in the driver's door. That is what Arthur had stumbled over on his way out of his truck. There were no fewer than eight loaded firearms from pistols to rifles all within Arthur's reach in the truck. In addition, there were five knives, a three-foot long machete that had been on the seat next to Arthur, and several other bladed weapons. Jay said that Arthur told him he wasn't going to be taken alive, that some cop would have to kill him first. Jay said it was fortunate that he was too drunk to get the .357 out of its holster, and that my repeated commands confused him enough that he left the cab with only the hunting knife. Otherwise, things could have ended very differently for both of us. I stared at the arsenal in Jay's car and listened to him from far away. I put on a smile and agreed that things had worked out fine, but deep down another emotion was brewing, but I wouldn't let it out. Not here, not now. It sunk back down.

Jay finished my MVA report and again thanked me for a job well done. He left me there on the road to wait for the tow truck. I didn't have long to wait. The NPS tow truck was down, so the concession tow truck arrived. We put my poor old car on a platform. I crawled up into the cab with the driver for the ride back to the Park. We traveled at a slow, 35 mph and had to avoid three elk on the road. I arrived back at the Park after 2:00 a.m. I removed all of the weapons and important items from the crunched Chevrolet and got back in my Caprice. I locked the weapons up in the safe at Ranger Operations, and went home. I couldn't help it. I woke up my Kent who was instantly awake and told him of my night. I just had to tell someone. He said he knew about the DUI, because he had been one of the Rangers heading out to back me up. I lay awake a long time that night.

The next morning, just about noon, there was a knock on the door. It was the District Ranger, who put out his hand to shake mine. He said don't worry about the car, those things happen … and thanks for not shooting "that guy" last night, the paperwork would have been something. With that he left. No "how are you," no "thanks for getting a drunk menace bent on killing people off the road," just thanks for minimizing the paperwork. This began a realization in me about my job and the things I do and who I do them for. It was a real eye-opener.

Later I called my Mom. I always called my Mom after big calls, and this one qualified. In addition to telling her about my night from hell, I told her about my frustrations and anger. I told her how mad I was to have been put in the position of deciding life or death. There is no doubt in my mind that I would have shot and killed Arthur if I had to. I was angrier with Arthur for putting me in that position and at the Park Service for not recognizing the position in which I had been placed. Oh well. As with so many things, I tucked it away and went on, until a funny thing happened.

The phone rang a few days later. It was my Dad. Now this was unusual. When I call home, my Dad's portion of the conversation usually consists of, "Hi honey, here's your Mom." One time, in college, I needed money and my Dad sent it with the note:

Here's the mon,
have fun,
hope you're glad,
dear old Dad.

So to have my Dad call me was something a little less common than asteroids hitting the earth! He said, "Your Mom said you had a rough night the other night and I called to see how you were doing."

That was it . . . the dam broke. The emotions I had buried on seeing Arthur's arsenal and the whole night's events came roaring to the surface and I did something I very rarely do. I cried. Not just little tears, I bawled my eyes out. I leaned against the wall as I told my Dad between sobs that I didn't want to kill the driver, I didn't want to die having almost been run over. I almost had to shoot him, and goodness knows what else. I think I caught my Dad off guard, as he didn't say much, just gave positive feedback of concern and reaffirming that I had done everything right and it had all turned out okay. This was my catharsis. Boy did I need that phone call. I thanked him, told him I loved him and that I was okay, and thanked him so much for calling, and hung up. No wonder he doesn't call much.

Epilogue

Arthur was arrested and charged with assault with a deadly weapon, aggravated DUI, and leaving the scene of an accident. The Superior Court of Arizona entered a plea bargain with Arthur, which found him guilty of one felony charge in exchange for dropping other charges. Arthur did not go to jail. Because he was a "model citizen" before this event, he was placed on probation and released. He is free today.

Cessna

The two-and-a-half hour search and rescue training on the rim of the Grand Canyon went well. There were many participants and we reviewed anchors, rigging, belays, rappels and so much more. For me though, the highlight was looking above at the California condors that hovered and circled mere feet above us. They are huge birds with nine-foot wingspans. It was so effortless for them to skim above us, to stay in the skies. Their dangling feet were comical and each had an easily identified wing number.

After a quick lunch, I went over to talk to Sally. Things were calm and very normal until the "high low" alert tone came over my hand-carried radio. I took the radio in my hand, anticipating a response to the tone, but there was a long pause of dead air space.

I remember saying out loud to the radio, "Come on Jay," (referring to the NPS Dispatcher on duty), "what have you got?" Then Jay said, to no one in particular, which was unusual, "Report of a Cessna that has crashed north of the South

Entrance Station."

I immediately requested a general alarm and went to my patrol car to head to Station 1. I thought it peculiar that Jay did not say, "a plane crashed," but that a "Cessna" had gone down. I later learned Jay had been on the red crash phone with the air traffic controller at the airport tower. They were the ones who said "Cessna" and had called initially when they thought the plane was in trouble. They kept Jay on the line as they watched the Cessna fall out of the sky and plummet into the ground. They told Jay what they saw and he repeated it verbatim to us.

A general alarm is basically an "all call" for all available rescue resources. Huge sirens, like the tsunami sirens in Hawaii, go off with a horrendous wail throughout the housing area. Then all of the pagers are activated. A few rangers go directly to the scene for a size up. All the rest go to Station 1. There we have two fire engines, Rescue 4 with extrication equipment, and two ambulances, referred to as Medics. I was so close; I was the third to arrive. I saw Medic 1 pull out and hoped those aboard had their personal protective equipment (PPE). Other names for the firefighting coat, pants, hood and gloves are turnouts and bunkers. You cannot hope to save someone if you yourself are injured. We are trained and know from experience that without PPE, you will burn to a crisp. Most airplane crashes in our experience do burn. Most car crashes do not. The percentages were on the side of a nasty fire.

As I pulled up to Fire Station 1, I turned off my lights and siren and put my defensive equipment in the trunk of my car and locked it. I entered Station 1, where there were two long rows of turnouts hanging from the walls. More and more persons came streaming in, including fire brigade members whose normal job was not protection. We have concession employees, a computer specialist, naturalists and others who are trained for these very incidents. I pulled off my uniform shirt and body armor, boots and pants and jumped into my bunker pants, pulling the red suspenders over my shoulders. Then I slipped the nomex hood over my head and threw my bunker jacket on and went to the front right seat of Engine 1. While I am often the engineer, I would be the Captain on this call. Michael, another engineer, came in and then Paul. Michael came to Engine 1 and Paul to Engine 2. I saw others and directed them to Rescue 4 and Medic 2. Within minutes we had a full crew and Michael pulled us out of the engine bay as I activated the siren and called on the radio that we were en route.

In the cab of the engine we wear headsets to protect ourselves from the siren noise and to communicate through an intercom system. With seat belts in place, everyone, including me, began to slip the straps of the self-contained breathing apparatus (SCBA) harness over our shoulders. The SCBAs were secreted in the hollow of our chairs so we could still sit back with them on. After securing the bright yellow tanks to our backs, we turned the regulator valve on and made sure the facemask on the low-pressure hose was attached and ready to go. In the back were Kristin, Colleen, Matt, and Jude. I asked them to buddy up and to be sure each team grabbed a tool as they exited. I assumed we would be one of the first crews in.

As we sped to the South Entrance Station, we were told that the crash was actually south of there. The first units arrived on scene and a call came over the radio: "One 901 and two alive."

It was amazing. Not that one was 901, our radio code for a dead person, but that two were actually alive! Eyewitnesses and bystanders had guided rescuers to the plane in the woods. One eyewitness was Don, our local electrician. Don later told how he had been leaving the airport going north and watched as the Cessna 177B had taken off. He remembered thinking that the engine rpm wasn't high enough and that they were way too low for a normal take off. As Don continued to drive onto the highway, he watched as the Cessna missed the Squire Inn by mere feet and then banked over the small grocery store. He knew it was in trouble then and thought the plane might try to land on the highway. Just short of the Forest Service housing area, the Cessna banked sharply and fell, shearing a four-foot diameter, hundred-foot tall pine in two. Then it plunged nose first into the ground.

Kent, the Fire Chief, arrived before us and, as we pulled up on scene, directed us to the staging area. As soon as the engine stopped, the four firefighters and I walked methodically up into the woods. Nobody ran. I could see a white color at first. As we got closer, the red, brown and white stripe and trim came into view. The plane was like a buried cross. The long, white wings were braced into the ground like outstretched arms and the body, from fuselage to the tail, pointed straight up into the air. The tail had broken off and was hanging like a guillotine blade.

I noticed that the Airport Fire Rescue truck was in the woods about fifty feet from the plane and that two of their firefighters, Tim and Robbie, had pulled a hose toward the plane. They had a foam application nozzle in their hands and, as I got closer, the smell of aviation gas was very strong. Under the right wing was the 901. Under the left wing trapped inside were two apparently alive but severely injured persons. I walked around the plane, seeing personal property, maps, a shoe, broken tree branches, fuel wetting the ground and another firefighter in PPE under the right wing. He was a volunteer named Andrew, who worked for the Forest Service. He pointed to a man below the craft and said, "He's dead." At Andrew's feet were three mass casualty tags, just lying before him as he knelt back on his knees. In front, mostly buried into the ground, making an eerie cast outline was the deceased male who had been the front right seat passenger of the plane. There were no cockpit controls and no engine ... they were off to the side. I later learned this man's name was Christian, and it was apparent from his injuries that he died instantly. His head was turned to the side and his body, well, I guess you could say, was crushed flat. Andrew said he could see through a small piece of the acrylic window that there was a woman trapped in the plane and that she appeared to be alive.

I walked to the left wing and asked the airport crew to start foaming the spilled fuel and the top of the wings. Foam acts as a barrier, to prevent fuel from rising and turning to vapor where it could ignite. Liquid fuel does not burn, but the invisible fumes evaporating from the liquid ignites and burns readily. Foaming really only works on level terrain because on a slope fuel can run out from underneath the static foam to release its vapors down the road.

The smell of gas was very strong and any spark could start a conflagration. I walked to the left wing and watched as the foam came spurting from the hose and began its cover-up of the fuel. I saw Matt below me and he pointed to the pilot, who was doubled up, chest over legs and pinned by his seat belt to the seat of the plane. He would be an easy extrication, under the circumstances, and I called for a backboard and more firefighters with PPE. I could see the pilot was unconscious and struggling to breathe. With each breath, his shirtless torso rattled and wheezed. I could see, too, that he was badly crushed and was covered in blood. There had to be a hole in his chest somewhere. With each breath I could hear air and gurgling from a sucking chest wound. As I got closer, I realized that what I thought was the back of his head was actually his now featureless face turned toward me. I later learned the pilot's name was Mike.

More firefighters arrived with the backboard and it was stationed beyond the wing. Mike's seat belt was released and his body supported and lowered, then turned face up. As he was pulled from the wreckage, his broken and bloodied body paraded past me. There were amputations and bone ends and a lifeless fall to his limbs. I not only instantly thought, "He's not going to make it," but hoped that he would not. He was placed on a backboard and carried the hundred yards to the waiting paramedics at the roadside.

Then we turned our attention to the woman. I looked in across what appeared to be an impossibly small place and saw her folded torso across thighs and legs with her head almost between her knees. Her eyes flickered and she was breathing. I stood up and turned my attention to the dangling tail. By this time, Kent had arrived with the rest of the crew and extrication equipment. I asked for bolt cutters. Patrick stood on the right wing with support and reached as high as he could with the cutters. Five of us supported the tail as he cut one, then another of the four wires holding the tail of the plane above us. When the last was cut, I expected a heavy weight, but the tail was surprisingly light, almost like a toy. It was downright flimsy. We carried it off to the side. Matt said that he thought the best access to the woman was through the belly of the plane. We lowered our face shields as

Paul stepped up with the *AMKUS* tool and pierced the metallic skin of the underbelly. He then manipulated the hydraulic-powered jaws to begin slicing. The hydraulic hoses were trailing off to the side and around to the generator. Chuck was behind Paul and kept them from getting tangled.

Then Kent came up with the air chisel. This would be faster. As he cut through and peeled back the frame, there was another layer. It was going to take too long this way. I asked Jude to re-evaluate the side of the craft where we took out Mike. He said he wasn't sure, but thought it was possible. I hung on to a wheel strut and lowered myself down and in. "Yes," I said, "we can do this."

We started a chain and pulled out debris, books, luggage, clothing and more, until I could see the woman more clearly. I thought if we could cut through the posts holding the pilot seat that had been displaced backward, we could pull it out and get to her. Paul lowered himself with the *AMKUS* tool as I removed my SCBA in anticipation of a tight fit. I crawled into the fuselage and tried to stand up, but ended up kneeling. I could touch her. I did.

She opened her eyes ... a flash of white in a red sea of blood on her face. She spoke ... in French. In the little French I knew, I asked her name. It was Celine. I asked how she was, and she said, "Fine," in French. It seemed so wrong for that word to come out of the mouth of this dangling bloodied woman ... but it did. I knew she was not totally with the program and was glad she could not feel most of her injuries. I continued to speak to her, told her who we were and that we would get her out. She didn't move, just closed her eyes. She couldn't move. She was wrapped pressed, contorted and locked into place by the wreckage all around her.

Paul cut the posts and the pilot's seat was pulled out. I touched what I could of her to give her comfort as the thumps and noise of the extrication echoed in that little space we were in. I looked up to see a large, car-sized battery hanging from its positive-pole cable. The negative was exposed. One spark, I thought, and those fumes will ignite into a fireball. I called out to Ronnie who was working a chisel through the top in case our side plan did not work. I had to yell out for him to stop because the chisel was so very loud. I just did not want any sparks . . . there was no way I could get out in time, let alone Celine. I had my turnouts on and my red fire helmet, but that would protect me for only so long. My bunkers were tan colored, made of a material called PBI, and had reflective stripes. My boots were rubber, and my fire resistant nomex hood covered my hair and ears, but not my face.

I touched Celine through my leather gloves and looked down to where I was kneeling. My right leg was on bent metal and wires and debris. My left leg was on less formidable debris. I looked down to see I was partially kneeling on Christian. There was nowhere else to go. I felt badly, for a moment. But I was able to tell myself that whatever it was that made that person alive and special was gone, and only the organic remained. At least his face was turned away from me.

I turned my attention back to Celine. Matt had worked his way into the makeshift doorway and had a backboard on the ground outside. More firefighters lined the board and it looked like we were ready to pull her out. I told Celine we were taking her out, and she opened her eyes and looked at me. I could only see her left eye clearly. Then I realized I was looking at her right eye through a tremendous gash through her upper eyelid. The laceration appeared to have grazed the eyeball in the upper orbit, missing the pupil and iris. She could still see through both eyes ... barely. I rose up and placed my left shoulder under her neck near her chest and reached up and unbuckled the tan and silver seat belt. She slid slowly onto my shoulder as I lowered myself, draping her upper body over me in a classic fireman's carry. Certainly it would have been nice to immobilize her spinal column and protect her neck, but we had no time. We were racing a clock attached to an invisible vaporous time bomb, not knowing when or if the fuel would ignite.

Holding her firmly, I asked her in French to lift her leg. She started to move her left leg and I reached down and pulled it free of the upholstery. Then I asked her to lift her right leg. She tried, but cried out in pain and could barely move it. I started to tug at it and realized her foot was more than just caught. It was a mess. She was in the inside of the plane, and her foot was on the out-side. Her lower leg was badly broken and dislocated and the foot partially amputated. Somehow it ended up outside, still attached, as the ripped metal of the side of the plane tried to cut it off during the impact.

I called out for help and Kristin crawled under the right wing where Andrew had been. I pulled on the seat back and made a small space as Kristin fed Celine's foot to me. It slowly emerged into view and the elastic skin of her leg tried to pull it back into its former shape. She still had her white sneaker on, with a hint of blood. As I looked at the separation of leg and foot, I immediately knew we were in trouble. It was not bleeding anymore. Either she had lost a tremendous amount of blood and had nothing left to lose – a process called exsanguination – or her blood pressure was so low from loss of blood that her heart did not have the power to pump what was left to her legs. Both scenarios were grim.

I was able to roll Celine over onto her back to Matt and together we worked her through the side of the plane to the waiting hands at the backboard. I crawled out and shakily stood up. I saw Nick, the Operations coordinator, and told him her status. Nick was not in PPE so was a distance away ... but yelling was still easier than trying to get a word in through the constant radio traffic. I told him I thought we should bring the helicopters and land them on the road. Nick replied that had already been done and that he wanted me to stay with the patient and fly with her to FMC, eighty miles away. I walked to the board and put my hands on either side of Celine's head to stabilize her neck. I turned to Kristin and Colleen and said, "Foam the heck out of this airplane."

We gingerly walked through the wreckage to a spot a hundred feet or so from the aircraft. There, the medical supplies, head blocks, and support straps had been staged. We set her down and, as she lay on her back, I knelt at her right side. Marty got a quick blood pressure as Brian set up to start an IV in her left arm. We placed a non-rebreather oxygen mask on her at 15 liters a minute, the highest possible. Marty said her blood pressure was 60 over nothing. When normal is 120 over 80, this was a bad sign. She needed fluids, oxygen and a surgeon. I took off my leather gloves and put on latex gloves. Marty stood up and walked away to get some equipment. Then the unthinkable happened.

There was a loud boom and an explosion! I quickly looked behind me and saw a huge cloud rushing through the air. My first thought was that the fuel tanks had ruptured and this was aviation gas vapor that would ignite at any moment; we would all be engulfed in a huge fireball. People were running past me to escape the explosive debris. I knew I had on PPE, but Celine did not. I threw myself across her torso and lay down on her to afford her some protection. I tightened my whole body, knowing any second shrapnel would pierce through my turnouts and impale themselves in my back. All of this took no time but lasted forever. The cloud descended over us.

With the most shock I had felt all day, I realized that it was not fuel vapor, but a fine white powder. My relief was instant and over just as quickly. The cloud got whiter and denser and sucked the air right out of the sky. I held my breath. I looked at Celine's oxygen mask and thought about borrowing it for just one breath. I couldn't. With the last bit of air in my lungs I burst out, "Grab the board ... let's go!" I could not even see my hand as I felt for the hold on the board and began lifting. I tilted the board. I could not lift it because I was by myself. I couldn't help it. I took a breath, a big one ... but there was no air. I tried again, nothing but the taste of a bitter-salty nature. I grabbed the board with both hands and tried to pull it, to drag Celine out. But my strength was gone and I could barely stand. I walked away from her and felt horrible, more for leaving her than for not being able to breathe.

As I walked toward the road, I found air coming into my lungs with each gasping breath. I called for a SCBA. I walked a few more steps and found three people who had escaped. I said, "Take some breaths and follow me back, we have to get her out of there." They ran while I stumbled behind them. We got to Celine as the cloud cleared and lifted her. Someone called out, "Take her all the way to the road." As we turned to walk, I could see back to where the plane was, and it was still there. It had not exploded ... what did? I feared I had been breathing in a hazardous material. What was that stuff doing to my lungs and my life? As we approached the road I saw Patrick. I told him to write down the names of everyone exposed ... and find out what it was.

We soon found out that the Airport Crash/Rescue truck had a 250-gallon cargo of extinguisher powder on board. It was powered through the charged hose by a high-pressure nitrogen cylinder. Apparently, the hose had failed with a loud boom and the contents of the cargo were released under high pressure into the air. It was a miracle it did not ignite the gas vapors. But no one could tell me what it was ... or if it was toxic.

We set Celine onto an ambulance gurney. I looked up and saw faces, familiar and not. I saw Steven and asked for an IV set up. Brian returned to start the IV in her left arm. I looked at her right arm and slipped an 18-gauge needle in a vein along her wrist. Once I pierced the skin, I advanced the plastic catheter over the needle to the hub, and then removed the needle. I gave the needle to Tim, the closest person, to dispose of in a sharps container. Marty hooked up the liter bag of 0.9% sodium chloride, normal saline, and squeezed the bag to give her the fluids her body needed so badly. I taped the IV in place, and listened to her lungs. They were remarkably clear. I pulled my trauma scissors out of my bunker pocket and made one cut down the side of her white knit shirt through her blue denim jumper.

Celine had huge bruises on either side of the front of her pelvic bone ... seat belt bruises. Her abdomen was firm but not tender. Her neck was intact with her trachea midline. Along both legs and arms she had cuts and bruises and large swollen areas.

But she could move all of her limbs on command. Her most obvious injuries were her face, eye, hips and lower right leg. It and the foot were splinted in a pillow. There was no pulse to the foot, but it still pinked up after the skin was blanched. Some circulation was getting there to continue to perfuse it. After applying head blocks, a cervical collar and restraining straps, we wheeled her toward the helicopter. Steven was placing the IV solutions into pressure bags to keep up the high flow during the flight. The EKG pads to the heart monitor would not stick because of all of the powder covering Celine.

Craig was waiting and would go with me to help with Celine's care. Eddie was the pilot. He was from New Zealand and was as good a pilot as they come. I entered the helicopter in the back right seat of the 407 model, and Craig sat in front of me, right behind Eddie with his back to the pilot. It was a tight fit. Celine lay on her backboard alongside us. Her head was even with mine. We had equipment stuffed everywhere. Craig's green medic bag was wedged between Celine's head and the chopper wall. The oxygen bottle was along her legs. The heart monitor was between the door and me, and the oxygen monitor was on Craig's lap. We could hardly move. Before we took off I told Eddie that I had no idea what the white powder was, so if he felt weird to let us know and we would give him the oxygen.

The doors were closed, the street was cleared and the rotors turned with a hum. There was a high pitch sound as the four blades began to circle and pick up speed. Then, with the familiar whup-whup and whirr, we began our lift off. Craig took another blood pressure and kept the IVs flowing. I began to notice more blood on her right shoe, and now blood was coming out of her torn eyelid and nostrils. Her pressure was at 100 systolic. That's good for perfusion, but bad if there are vessel breaks. If we got her pressure up too high, she could bleed out. It was a tricky balance to keep the IVs going at a rate to maintain good perfusion, but not so high as to exsanguinate the patient. We applied pressure as needed, and I noted how much more swollen her right eye and face were becoming. She had a huge shiner. In fact, we perfused her so well that with her increased alertness came pain. She told me how her leg and foot hurt. There is no way I could give her pain meds in the field with her multisystem trauma and low blood pressure. It could mask life-threatening signs and symptoms. I guess it is better to feel pain than nothing at all.

Eddie fixed the radio channels so I could call the Emergency Room at FMC. We had a 25-minute ETA. I told them my twenty-two-year-old female was the first of two patients they would receive from this plane crash. I put them on standby as Craig motioned to me. He told me on the intership communications system (ICS) that the pilot had died. Within minutes of pulling him from the wreckage, he had stopped breathing, then coded. CPR and advanced life support could not overcome the severity of his injuries. I passed that information on to the ER and finished my call. I felt tired and had a headache. I felt that it was a miracle that Celine had survived this long, and I briefly thought she would not make it because her two companions had died. But I had work to do, and Craig and I began to do it. We reapplied the EKG pads, put her on the oxygen monitor, fixed her IV lines, replaced her almost spent oxygen cylinder, took vital signs and controlled bleeding. We replaced her oxygen mask. If the powder was toxic, we wanted to minimize her exposure to it. I spoke to her and we took turns trying to hold her hand.

I asked our pilot Eddie through the ICS how much longer. There was no answer. I tried again, and he still didn't answer me. I looked up toward him and he was sitting still with his head slightly bent down. I asked Craig if he could hear me in the ICS and Craig said yes. I heard him clearly, so he tried to call Eddie on the ICS. There was still no answer and Eddie didn't move. Craig turned to look at me as I was now sitting very upright in my chair. Forget the ICS. I yelled as loud as I could, "Eddie!" and still nothing. The powder I know how to turn a helicopter off, but I certainly don't know how to fly one or keep one in the air. My headache got very bad very quickly. Craig turned and reached into the pilot's compartment and squeezed Eddie's left shoulder. He almost launched him. Eddie jerked up and out of his seat with the most startlement I have ever seen in a surprised person.

"Bloody hell," Eddie said in the ICS, as he half turned around in his seat. "You scared the sh-- out of me!"

"*You* were scared," I replied. "You didn't answer us on the ICS ... we thought you were going into a coma or something."

"You two were talking so much on the ICS that I turned mine off," he replied.

Craig interjected, "But your head was pointed down like you were asleep!"

"My head is down 'cause that's where the bloody instruments are!" Eddie responded.

His tone was less angry and startled and more relieved. My headache did not go away, but it got a lot better. But I still didn't feel 100%. I was not going to talk myself into anything. I was going to be fine. Sigh.

We made our approach to the helicopter landing pad on the

roof of FMC. The landing was flawless and we waited the three minutes for the engine to cool before we shut it down. The ER staff arrived with a gurney. Through the gowns, masks and goggles, I recognized Beth, an RN I work with in the ER, and Seth, one of the technicians. We transferred Celine's oxygen line and lifted her to the gurney, covering her with a blanket. Across the helipad we rolled the gurney through puddles of water from a recent downpour. I heard thunder in the distance. Despite being outside in the cool crisp air, I was hot. We went into the elevator, down to the first floor and over to decontamination. It was adjacent to the trauma rooms. Celine was still talking to me in French and seemed to be stable.

As we entered the decontamination room, I began to give my report, but paused to catch my breath. Dr. Mike looked up at me. He was in gown, gloves and mask. He looked at me with concern and asked me if I was okay. He said I was beet red and diaphoretic (all wet from perspiration). I totally surprised myself and answered, "No," and left the room.

I started to see sparkles and was determined not to lose it. I knelt down to put my head between my knees and another RN, Shelly, came over. With Eddie, she helped me off with my turnout coat. I felt cooler, but sick. They helped me to lie down on a gurney and Shelly gave me an oxygen mask. I felt better and better. After taking my vital signs and turning down an offer to be checked in, I sat up and in about five minutes was my old self. Even my headache was gone, but I was dripping wet in my bunkers. Craig got off the phone with Dispatch where he learned the nature of the white powder. It was sodium bicarbonate, an agent kept in extinguishers and used to put out fires by smothering them. I can testify to the efficiency of that aspect. It can cause irritation to the respiratory tract if inhaled, and eye and skin irritation. It sounded benign, but at the time of exposure, it seemed so much more.

Shelly brought me juice and I thanked her as I went to Trauma 3 to give my report. Celine was still alive and speaking in French to an interpreter. I learned she was from Switzerland, and that Christian was her boyfriend and Mike was his cousin. Mike had rented the plane in California and they flew here to see the canyon. Celine let Christian sit in the front seat of the plane for a better view because she had seen the canyon once before. We did not tell her they had died. She had too many other things to worry about.

Celine went to surgery where they successfully reattached her foot and lower leg. They also discovered multiple facial fractures, including a bone displacement that created a hole below her right eye orbit. But they could not fix that for several days because she took a turn for the worse after her first surgery and was admitted to the Intensive Care Unit. Her family arrived two days later and she had stabilized enough to return to surgery the next day. While she sustained critical injuries, she was expected to fully recover physically.

We waited out a thunderstorm at FMC before Eddie was able to fly us back to the canyon. Nearing our destination, we circled the crash site. I looked down at the wreckage and wondered how anyone could have survived. The Cessna stood like a cross in the wilderness.

Screamer

The day before had been a nightmare, and a long one. An 18-wheeler carrying ice tipped its load onto a motorhome on a curve at Desert View. The load crushed the motorhome, killing the driver and his wife and severely injuring others. Hazardous materials were spilled, extrication occurred and the day's work lasted more than twelve hours. Today was regroup.

While clean up occurs immediately after all calls, fatigue and lack of supplies all contribute to incomplete restocking of rigs. I had completed an overhaul of Rescue 4 and its extrication and mass casualty kits as well as the equipment on Engine 1, including the firefighting tools and SCBAs. I was halfway through the two ambulances when a call came in for a 33-foot raft, stuck and wedged on rocks in the middle of Crystal Rapids on the Colorado River, downstream from Phantom Ranch. They needed all available swiftwater trained SAR as well as helicopter shorthaul personnel. I was on both teams, so received a release from my south rim duties and headed for the helibase. It was noon, so I wouldn't have lunch. I found an energy bar and ate half of it on the way. Then I concentrated on pre-hydrating. It's usually hot on the shore adjacent to the river. Today it was 110 degrees in the shade. It would be much hotter in the sun.

I was the first to arrive and reported to the SAR shift person, Mike, who would be the Incident Commander (IC). We were incredibly shorthanded. Since the summer before, we had lost seventeen rangers to transfers and changes in status. Only two of those positions had been filled. Mike knew this and went to the extreme, asking for a general alarm and asking again for all technically trained persons to respond. More began to trickle in. As I changed into my SAR gear, Mike filled us in.

This was a commercial river trip with seventeen people on board. The river water had been running low, as it would for some time. This made the river much more treacherous, and we knew that this might happen. The lower the river, the more exposed the rocks became and the worse the rapids, as the water went through narrower passages. In fact, one other boat had already become stuck just ten days before, but they were able to get free by shifting gear and changing the weight distribution of the raft. This one didn't sound as if it would be so lucky.

One of the Rescue Rangers, Bil, was already in the helicopter on a non-urgent mission. As we pulled out our rescue gear and began to prepare a plan, Bil was sent by the IC, Mike, to scout the river and the raft. The word came back from Bil by radio that the raft was truly stuck and would not be coming off on its own. It appeared stable and at this time, no one was reporting any injuries. Bil was put down on the sandy beach upstream and north of the raft's position on Crystal Rapids. The ship returned for the rest of us.

I called home and asked my husband Kent if he could bring

my two wetsuits. He did. It may sound peculiar to want two wetsuits; in this case a shorty (short arms and legs) and a farmer john (long legs and no arms), but I had learned my lesson during swiftwater training at Badger Rapids.

In order to be able to do what we do, we must train and be confident and proficient in the rescues we perform. So, in swiftwater training, we go to the maximum to put ourselves into dangerous and compromising situations to give us the knowledge and confidence of self-rescue. Once we can do that, it's a small step to rescuing others in the water. That way, we are thinking more about the circumstances and the people to be rescued instead of whether we are capable of surviving if we are thrown into the river while rescuing others.

Training starts with a lot of classroom work, diagrams and discussions. Then the chairs are pushed aside and we set up pulley systems, tie knots and rig for rescue, learning about all of the equipment. The next step is at the Colorado River itself. In a relatively calm area without rapids but with a fast current, we would position ourselves on the side of the river near Lee's Ferry, upstream from a large rock in the middle of the river, which is several hundred feet across. A zip line is set up from the rock to the shore, downstream. Persons with throw bags are positioned along the shore and more with kayaks are farther downstream. The plan is to jump into the water, and swim as hard as you can for the rock. The rock creates an eddy or reverse current behind it. Once you near the rock, you break through the wall of the two currents any way you can, and then easily climb onto the rock. Throw bags are held by rescuers on shore. There are two for each station. If a trainee is swept past the rock, a bag with coiled rope is thrown toward the trainee, accounting for drift. If they catch it, they hang on and the current pendulums them to shore, or they are hauled in if there are enough persons on the haul line. The kayakers are sort of a last hope. Should a person not break through the eddy and be too far or past the throw rope stations, the kayakers head toward the drifting and rapidly disappearing swimmer. We are trained to hang on only to the back pointed tail of the kayak. If we were to throw ourselves across its main body, we could swamp and or overturn it; both kayaker and swimmer would be in the same boat ... or out of it in this case. Finally, we are trained to self-rescue. If possible, as we are carried downstream in the current, we float on our back and point our feet downstream. That way if we hit a rock or other object, our feet, not our head, would take the blow. When strength and opportunity are both present, we begin actively swimming upstream toward a side. This way our feet are still first, and we are beginning to slide sideways, despite our downstream drift in the swift current. Hopefully we have aimed for an eddy curtain and when we get to it, we break through and begin a slower swirl in the opposite direction than the main river toward shore. Knowing you can save yourself when all other help is incapable of reaching you is an incredibly powerful mental edge to surviving rapids and swift currents during a rescue operation.

I worked the shore side of the zip line for a while, watching as rescuers in training threw themselves into the river and swam for the rock. Many broke through the eddy fence to climb up onto the rock, many were repelled. Some were picked up by the kayakers and others self-rescued. Once they got onto the rock, they placed their wrist through a handhold and lowered themselves into the water. The swift current caught them and they zipped across the current as they headed downstream to the shore and to me. I helped them to unhook. It was my turn to rotate to the upriver shore entry point. Very quickly the need for wetsuits became apparent. The Colorado River is a cold, 48 degrees Fahrenheit. Historically, it had been in the 80's in the summer, but the construction of Glen Canyon Dam changed that. Now, water is released from the bottom of the dam and remains cold for the majority of the trip to Lake Mead at Hoover Dam. Fish that loved the warm, muddy water became fewer or disappeared. Introduced trout replaced the endemic chub. The non-native trout love the cold, clear water, and bald eagles that just flew by in the past, now stop to feast on the trout. It has created a whole new ecology. But the cold is very real. I had on two wetsuits, a shorty and a thin full suit, booties, gloves and a hood. On the hood I had a climbing helmet. I entered the water and swam for the rock. It was much faster and colder than I expected. It initially took my breath away but I swam on. I went past the rock and, at the eddy fence, pulled with all of my might and flipped onto my back as I had seen others do before me. Much to my surprise, I was not behind the rock, but was swiftly coursing downstream in the middle of the river, too far for any throw bags. A kayaker made a beeline to me and, as we had trained, I maneuvered behind and grabbed onto the tail. I kicked to help with the kayaker's steady paddle work. I was mortified I had not made it through the eddy fence. He helped me to shore and I walked upstream to the input area. The cold no longer a factor, all but forgotten in the determination I was mustering to do it right. I waited my turn as others ahead of me put in. More and more were consistently making it through the eddy fence and onto the rock. We were going in twos now. I crouched among the dried bushes that lined the shore, the sand muddy from the dripping of wetsuits. Then in. I swam with strength and purpose. This time no fancy flips. As I approached the eddy fence, I powered my way through. I felt my body surge, then lift and turn over on its own. I was in the eddy. I learned that the eddy makes you flip, that trying to flip prematurely only makes you lose the penetration speed necessary to cross the wall of water. With great relief and an ear-to-ear grin, I climbed up onto the rock.

When it came my turn for the zip line, I put my wrist through the loop and lowered myself into the water. It was a bit rough, but the current was relentless as it powered me down river and across to the shore. Halfway through the trip, my arm and shoulder began to ache with the strength it took to hold on. I made it to shore, but with a new realization at how much muscle it took to do a lot of this. I was one of three women at this training; the rest were men. We were all in good shape and counting on each other. We de-rigged, had a review of the day, ate dinner and went to bed for the night. The next day would be the real test . . . at Badger Rapids.

Again we met at the boat ramp at Lee's Ferry. It was a cool morning. Powerboats arrived to take us downstream to Badger Rapids. Badger is almost eight miles downstream from Lee's Ferry. Badger Canyon and Jackass Creek enter at this point and its runoff of rocky debris and boulders has narrowed the main channel, making the water go through more rapidly than at a wider point, hence the term rapids. Rapids are generally rated from 1-10 in the Grand Canyon, with "10" being the most severe. There is such a rapids on the river. It's called Lava Falls and it is rated a "10," falling thirty-seven feet. Badger is "5-8" depending on the flow of the river water. The lower the flow the more severe the rapid, as rocks are exposed and then passages become more narrow and severe. Badger falls about fifteen feet in the one- to two-hundred-yard length course. It's one of the nastier rapids, but not the worst. I have been through Lava in a big Park Service boat and it was a kick of a ride, but over quickly. Badger looked longer to me. But then, maybe that was because I would be going through it without a boat. We were dropped off on the south side of the river. We climbed up the cliffs and talked about what we saw. We climbed down, walked downstream alongside the rapids, scouted it, read it, listened to it and felt the pounding surge of its crashing waves beat into our chests. As I walked back upstream through the sand and shrubbery, I began to review just why I was doing this: to help others, of course.

As I climbed over the dark, slick rocks to the waiting motorboat, I watched as groups ahead of me began their passage. Our small group of four, plus an instructor, met at the edge of the river. The engine on the powerboat was working hard to keep its place in the water. Should it quit, all there would be on the other side of the rapids was toothpicks. There were too many exposed rocks for a wooden boat of this build to survive intact.

We again reviewed. Aim for the tongue, the rising wall of water at the heart of the rapid. Stay away from the rooster tail to the right. Entering that meant severe bodily harm because you would be dashed onto rocks and then spit out. Stay away from the hole on the left. It looked so innocent, a smooth cascade of water over a rock and up another, falling back on itself. This reverse hydraulic was deadly. Get caught in there and you would be churned around and around and pinned to the bottom. You would not be spit out, you would become trapped and that meant certain death. This review was making what we were doing very, very real. This training was not your average, give it a try, and if you mess up, try it again. If you messed up ... well, you get the idea.

I will admit that as I stepped onto the boat there was a brief moment of great fright, a sort of "what the hell am I doing here" feeling. I was afraid. But as I turned to look at the rapids, that feeling went away as quickly as it had come. I read the rapids. I saw the hole and the rooster tail. I saw the tongue. I knew what I was doing and I knew what to do here. We stepped onto the transom, the rear platform of the boat. The craft was pointed upstream, the motor screaming to keep it in place with just a slow backward drift. Then we heard the word, "GO!"

We all jumped in the river. I swam as I had never swum before. I watched the tongue and I swam for it with all of my might, kicking, pulling, straining. I didn't even notice the frigid water. Then I was in. I was carried higher and higher into and over the entry tongue, up the side of the mountain, then crashing down the other. I was in the rapids. I worked to keep my feet downstream and my head up, but it was almost impossible. It was like some invisible force kept pulling my feet back down. Waves crashed over my head from all directions. I turned my head to the side to breathe as I had been taught. There was air. I sucked it in. It worked.

Like a cork I bobbed through the rapids and incredibly over the roar of the waves, I heard my name. It was Steven, part of my jump group. He asked if I was okay. I said yes, and asked him the same. He said yes. We both grinned at each other. We were okay, we were managing just fine, and it just occurred to us that we were having the ride of our lives. We tried to stay near each other but in another few seconds, we were separated by the roller coaster waves. As they became less and less powerful, I looked around. I could see the shore and people on it. I picked out the rest of my jump group. Some were ahead of me and some were behind. I saw rescuers on the shore down river with throw bags. I saw kayakers. I floated. I was fine.

We got the signal from the instructor to start for shore. I began my ferry angle of swimming diagonally across the current toward an eddy. As I worked hard at swimming, a kayaker came by and offered me a lift. I smiled and said, "No, thank you," and he said, "Way to go," paddling on to check on others. I swam and swam and made it to the eddy fence. I pushed through and slowed in the upstream current. Quickly I felt bottom, and stood up. I walked out onto the shore ... myself ... all by myself. No matter what happened on any rescue in the future, I knew I would survive. I could self-rescue.

If you think that is not crazy enough, we did it again! Then we got into small rubber boats ... four of us in each. We paddled like mad for the tongue and, at the top of the tongue, flipped the boat on purpose. We were training ourselves. I hung onto my paddle. I came up under the boat for air in the middle of the rapids. I dove back down, surfaced next to it and climbed onto the bottom of the overturned boat. I pulled myself on it through sheer upper body strength ... there was no good purchase in the rapids to kick against. With the other team members who also clamored aboard, we flipped it right side up. I helped to pull others in. We self-rescued. We did it again. We were good. You know you are comfortable when, on the last boat flip, you are talking about what's for dinner instead of how the logistics of the rescue went. It was second nature now. But just under the surface, among the camaraderie and laughter, we all knew just how difficult this was – how our lives and the lives of others depended on our skill, knowledge and training.

Now, at the South Rim Helibase with my two wetsuits from Kent, shorthaul equipment, medical equipment and SAR gear, I was ready for the Crystal Rapids mission. It was not supposed to involve swiftwater rescue, but it could end up that way. We went prepared.

Like so many shorthaul rescues, it all depended on teamwork and training. We would have a briefing, assignments would be given, and the logistics would be discussed. Safety is always first. We have a mantra … you cannot help anyone if you become a victim yourself. It is their emergency, not yours. We walk fast, rarely run. We repeat communications to be sure we understand. We place human beings as radio relays so all know what is happening. With people in the water, things are stepped up and not as clean, but we still understand our role. I was once on a mission when a boat flipped and people were in the water and trapped under the raft. On our arrival, we commandeered private boats in the area and picked up persons in the water like apples from a barrel. Luckily, the worst trauma was a broken wrist. But several were suffering from hypothermia caused by exposure to the 48-degree water. Can you imagine dying of the cold when it's over 120 degrees outside? The solution was quick and repeated for each victim. Get them out of the water and onto the shore. They would warm up quickly enough, and they did.

On this mission, all persons were still on the boat. I was one of two rescuers who would shorthaul to the raft, check for injuries and assist in off-loading passengers by helicopter. Shorthaul is fun, if you don't mind heights and speed. You wear a chest and seat harness and two pieces of sewn webbing material that you hook onto a ring from a line below the helicopter. The line from the chopper is one hundred feet long and the rescuer is on the end of it, sometimes alone, sometimes with another rescuer or with a patient. The latter was often secured inside a body-long basket.

In my early training, Jerry, a great pilot, loved to fly us through the air at sixty miles an hour. We would lift off, circle the trees of the helibase, and practice pinpoint landings on the ground, hooking up and hooking off of the shorthaul line. You are trained to always watch the chopper at these times. If it suffers a catastrophic failure, it will come down on you like a brick, a very big and heavy brick. So you need to know which way to run or dive.

We are also trained in parachute landings and releasing ourselves from the helicopter if it falls into the river on a rescue. In training, you are dumped into a pool with all of your gear on, including helmet. First, you release your radio line from your helmet. Then you release your seat belt with one hand, keeping your other on the door so you can feel your way out. You count and wait for the rotors to stop so you don't get your head chopped off, and crawl out to the bottom and swim to the top.

But there is nothing like a real mission. It's one thing to be 300 feet off of the ground during practice, but the first time I went from the rim to over the Grand Canyon, it was incredible. With over 5,000 feet between you and the ground, 100 feet up to the belly of the helicopter, and all that is holding you there is a rope, well, let's just say it makes your heart beat a little bit faster. It is an awesome experience and when I had the opportunity to fly, I felt almost privileged to be in my position.

One mission, on the Hance Trail, came in as a call for a woman who fell while backpacking in a rugged and remote area of the canyon. The initial report said that she was alive but that there was possible brain matter exposed. It was almost sunset and our helicopter was not available. If the report was true, she wouldn't last the night and it would take hours for a medic to hike to her. We had trained with the Arizona DPS and it was decided we would use their ship, pilot and spotter. We rangers would be the medics.

Tammy and I were both paramedics and were prepared to fly. The DPS helicopter arrived and landed on the roadway called East Rim Drive. Traffic was stopped and we briefed with the pilot and spotter. The spotter is the team member who is in the back of the helicopter. It's their job to be another set of eyes for the pilot, to communicate with the shorthaul team members on the rope, and to release the rope from the ship should it become necessary. While we don't relish the idea of being cut loose while dangling from the helicopter, it is a possible outcome if a hazard occurs that makes it a necessity. For example, if the ship loses power and they need to jettison weight to try to safely land, we are jettisoned. We even carry quick release knives to jettison ourselves. But that is only done if the ship is about to crash or crashes and we are being dragged. We do train for all of these contingencies and realize the risks.

After our briefing the ship, with its doors off and bellyband in place, was connected to the shorthaul line. Then it began to lift straight up off of the ground. Tammy and I intently watched the ship and spotter. As soon as it held hover, we were given the okay to move under the ship to the line. Attached to us were oxygen cylinders, medic bags, a collapsible backboard and bag for enclosing the patient, suction, webbing and equipment to survive the night if needed. We also had our jackets on. It was a cold time of the year with patchy snow and when flying through the air outside of the ship, the wind chill could be brutal. We both had flight helmets on and I was connected to the radio communications with the ship. Because there was only one radio jack, I would have to yell to Tammy what was going on. The flight would be short, about four to five minutes: over the rim, down the saddle and past the trail to the wash where our patient and her party were waiting. Within ten seconds I knew something was wrong.

Instead of the quick drop and sideslip to the saddle, we were headed at great speed straight over the canyon toward the Colorado River. Tammy and I both looked up at out spotter, but he was not looking at us. We strained and tried to will the spotter to look down at us, but he didn't look down. In our system we are trained to make eye contact every thirty seconds to a minute and to signal all is okay by tapping one open hand on the top of our helmet. The spotter mimics our gesture assuring us they saw we are okay. Tammy and I both knew this canyon very well and we knew this was not the way to the patient. The DPS crew was not from the canyon and I feared they did not know where they were going. I tried the radio, but the wind was blowing so hard, they couldn't hear me and I couldn't hear them. We continued to look up to the spotter, but he still hadn't looked down to us. We were flying miles from the south rim, thousands of feet above the ground, hanging from a rope below a ship with a crew that appeared to be lost. I started to get chilled, and I wasn't sure it was all from the wind. Tammy, screaming over the wind was asking me what in the world was going on. I could see she was unsettled, and I decided to lie.

"They are going the long way around the butte for a better approach."

She quickly answered, "Oh," and seemed to make an expression of exasperation as if to say, there is an easier way, but oh well.

I looked all around me and was so much more aware of my surroundings then ever before. A peace came over me as I watched the incredible pink hues of the sunset in the west and the incredible visage of the full moon rising in the east. I will always remember that moment. It told me that I had better just enjoy the ride and stay calm because I wasn't in a position to do anything about it. Indeed, it was a rather fateful feeling, a sort of *que será, será*. If the rope was to go, a fall was not survivable so we had to just sit back and relax. That is exactly what I did.

It was the longest shorthaul of my career: seventeen minutes. We went within spitting distance of the river, around a butte and up the canyon. We found the party with the injured person, but they were in a narrow canyon. As the pilot lowered us down, the ship drifted and both Tammy and I were suddenly slammed into the jutting rocks of a wall as we were lowered. I'm afraid Tammy took the harder hit. She later told me she was sore for a long time. We landed, unhooked in record time and began to assess and package the patient while the ship backed off until we were ready. Luckily, the patient was not as badly injured as first reported and could actually talk to us ... in German. I got my suction ready and pulled the straps of the litter and bag together as the ship came back in. I would fly out with the patient and Tammy would hike out, painfully. Our ground time was just over seven minutes and the flight out only four minutes ... as it should have been on the way in. The patient ended up recovering completely from her fall, but I never recovered from one of the most incredible views and experiences of my life.

Back at the beach, we could see the raft that was wrapped around the rock. Dave assessed the situation. Dave is the strongest person I know. He is all muscle. He is the lead river boatman, knows this river better than anyone, and spends his life rowing on it as a River Patrol Ranger. He felt that the boat, a large inflatable with gray pontoons, would work its way off the rock if we off-loaded passengers and shifted gear around.

We geared up. First he, then I were lifted to the boat in the middle of the river. This was good and not so good. It was so hot on the beach with a wet suit on that I was dunking myself in the river to keep from getting heat stroke while I waited. When I was lifted into the air, sand from the beach was blowing everywhere, despite our efforts to water it down. The pilot skillfully maneuvered me over the boat and slowly lowered me to the box between the pontoons. There was some drift and I began to slide toward the river. But he slid sideways and I was on the deck, eyes riveted on the ship as I disconnected. I brought helmets and equipment for off-loading the passengers. Once on the boat, the wind generated by the river rushing by made it tolerably cooler, but the raft was continuously being banged and buffeted by the waves in the rapids, jostling things around and making communication difficult.

As planned, Dave met with the boatman and the swamper, the crew whose job it was to do all of the odds and ends tasks on the boat and on the trip. I turned my attention to the fifteen people huddled down in the bottom of the craft, who were anxious to hear the plan. They saw how Dave and I arrived, and I could tell some were not too excited about getting off the raft in that manner. I gave a short safety speech and told them the plan: that they would be shorthauled to the beach and spend the night there. If all went according to plan, they would reboard their boat and continue their trip in the morning. There were a few questions. I explained the gear and told them Dave and I would "dress" them, sending them off in pairs. They were not to bring any gear other than a fanny pack and a camera ... their hands had to be free to assist.

Since this mission we have graduated to a fabric triangle for offloading passengers, a big piece of sewn material that a person wears like a diaper. The three ends come together to hook into the shorthaul line. But on this mission, we had screamer suits. They were made of mesh with straps and were big enough to accommodate all sizes of passengers with their personal flotation device on. We actually called them screamer suits. When a passenger asked me why, I said it was because passengers often cry out with excitement the first time they shorthaul. She gave me a dubious look.

I dressed the first two passengers with helmets and screamer suits and Dave dressed another two. The first set of gear would return with the line so we would always have two passengers "good to go." Dave did the communication, marshalling the chopper in. He got the line and I motioned the hunched passengers to stand while we clipped them in. Dave motioned for the ship to go and, with a quick uplift, they were off the boat. In their wake were a pair of lustful, full-body screams.

I smiled and looked at Dave who laughed heartily. It's always the first two who scream, not realizing what to expect. The rest of the passengers, hearing this, go to great lengths not to scream like the first two ... not all are successful. Some are so cool about it, they take pictures during their flight. On shore there was a team member who unhooked the passengers and directed them up a small side canyon to safely wait until the mission was over.

Finally, all the passengers were off-loaded and their gear was on the shore. We bagged it up into nets and sent it over for the night. The boatman would stay on board until the boat shifted and would direct it to a cove for reboarding in the morning. I was shorthauled back to the shore after thirty minutes on the boat, quickly took off my personal flotation device and peeled off my wetsuit. We gathered our gear and were flown back to the South Rim for hours of cleaning, getting sand out of gear, drying equipment and repacking. Damn, that was fun.

A Moment

The area near the South Kaibab Trailhead has a cliff that falls straight down for 400 feet to the limestone and shrubs below. We had spent all day and part of the night training for vertical, high-angle technical rescues. A team member, braver than I, agreed to be strapped into the rescue litter and lowered over this edge so we could practice hauling them up and over. The coordinator made assignments and set us to task. Holes were drilled for anchor bolts. Webbing and pre-tension back ties were placed. Belay lines were established. The "patient" was packaged and gently lowered over the edge to dangle in mid-air. When all was ready, we would switch from the lower lines to the raising lines, and bring the "patient" up.

"Again," the coordinator would implore. We derigged and started all over. This time, we used pulleys and z-rigs instead of a mechanical assist device ... and a new "volunteer victim."

"Again."

It was almost midnight by the time we finished. We wanted to practice at night because victims do not always conveniently fall during the day. We wanted to use a large cliff face so we had to be careful and had to take it seriously. There is absolutely no goofing off in training when one of your team members is over a four-hundred-foot ledge. But we were also there for the reward.

When we were done, those who wanted were given the opportunity to rappel down the four-hundred-foot cliff in the dark, walk cross-country, pick up the trail and walk back up to the training site. Few turned down the opportunity.

I was the second one over. I had my helmet with a headlamp, seat and chest harness, rappel rack and ascenders, the latter just in case I had to come back up the rope. I also had a chemical light attached to my harness so I could be seen at a distance. I placed my rope through the rappel rack and went on belay. This is a second rope managed by a belayer whose job is to hold you if your primary rappel rope failed. I turned on my light, stepped back over the edge and could see just the faintest speck of a chemical light from the person four hundred feet below me and off to the side. I walked down the face until it curved under the cliff and was gone. I was dangling in mid air, using my rappel rack to lower to the ground below. I could make out the cliff face in my headlamp about twenty feet away. When I was halfway down, I decided to stop. I locked down my rack, called up "tension on belay," so they wouldn't pay out any more rope, and turned off my headlamp. The chemical light was distracting so I stuffed it in my shirt and slowly swiveled on my lines, two hundred feet in the middle of total darkness. It was like being in a cave at first. Then as my eyes adjusted, the stars, so brilliant in the thin air from 7,000 feet, began to become more apparent. In a short time, the incredible night sky and the depth of my position in time and space overwhelmed me. For just a moment, I was the luckiest person in the world.

12-lead – an electrocardiogram of the heart that looks at it electronically from many angles. A myocardial infarction may be detected from a 12-lead EKG.

901 – code use over the radio to indicate a dead body.

AC – antecubital space on the arm where large veins can be found for establishing IVs.

ACLS – advanced cardiac life support which includes EKG monitoring, 12-lead EKG, and associated cardiac medications.

advanced cardiac life support – see *ACLS.*

advanced life support – see *ALS.*

ALOC – altered level of consciousness; a patient who is altered can be disoriented, combative or near coma.

ALS – advanced life support; medical intervention beyond the basic level which includes intravenous lines, advanced airway management, and administering medications. These skills are performed by Intermediate EMTs and paramedics.

Altered level of consciousness – see *ALOC.*

AMKUS **tool** – extrication tool that works on hydraulics and a portable compressor. It is also called the jaws of life.

arêtes – sharply-edged peaks formed by the carving of a glacier.

bash pack – a small search and rescue pack with all the necessary equipment for two rescuers to immediately begin a technical climb or rescue.

basic EMT – Basic Emergency Medical Technician can provide basic life support through stabilization and transport of patients.

Beck's triad – identifies a pericardial tamponade as plummeting systolic blood pressure and rising diastolic pressure, muffled heart tones, and blood backing up in the veins that transport blood to the heart.

betadyne – an antimicrobial iodine-based cleanser.

BLS – Basic life support or EMT skills.

bunkers – see *turnouts*.

called the code – to stop all efforts to revive a patient after medical intervention has been unsuccessful.

catheter – a sterile plastic tube with a needle in the center. The needle is used to enter the skin and vein and is removed after the plastic tube is advanced into the vein. It is used for the administration of fluids and IV medications .

charged line – an extended fire hose that has received water under pressure from a fire engine.

coded – slang for a patient with no respiration and no pulse; clinical death.

code 3 – driving emergency vehicles with lights and sirens and as quickly as is safe.

code 4 – radio communication indicating all is okay.

command – in the hierarchy of the ICS system, the person in charge of the entire incident. Also known as the incident commander.

coronary arteries – the arteries that supply and perfuse the heart muscle, circling around like a crown or coronation.

CPR – cardiopulmonary resuscitation.

DPS – Department of Public Safety.

decompression of tension pneumothorax – see *needle thoracostomy*.

diaphoretic – sweating profusely.

diastolic blood pressure – the lower number in a blood pressure reading indicating the resting pressure of the heart.

EKG – Electrocardiogram, the electronic monitoring of the heart.

electrocardiogram – see *EKG*.

Emergency medical technician – see *EMT*.

EMS – Emergency medical services.

EMSCOM – emergency medical service communication; a system for talking by telephone or radio to a base station physician.

EMT – Emergency Medical Technician, a trained medical professional in basic life support.

ETA – estimated time of arrival.

exsanguination – total loss of blood, bleeding out.

flail chest – when trauma causes three or more ribs on one side to be broken in two or more places. A flail chest disrupts the integrity of the chest cavity making breathing inefficient and difficult.

FMC – Flagstaff Medical Center.

general alarm – an all call for all available personnel to respond to a major incident or an emergency. It involves radio tones, pager activation and siren activation.

gpm – gallons per minute.

ICS – Incident command system; the organizational system used to coordinate and treat any large or involved incident or emergency.

I-EMT – Intermediate (I) Emergency Medical Technician can provide advance life support by starting IVs, establishing advanced airways and administering some medications.

Incident command system – see *ICS*.

ischemia – lack of blood supply to tissues resulting in low oxygen and possible tissue damage.

IV – intravenous is a medical access to a patient through a catheter to deliver fluids and medications directly into a patient's veins.

Jugular venous distension – see *JVD*.

JVD – jugular vein distension; caused when there is increased pressure in the chest backing blood into these neck veins. It can be a sign of pericardial tamponade or tension pneumothorax.

lactated Ringer's – an intravenous solution that replaces fluids and electrolytes.

LZ – landing zone (usually for helicopters). A helicopter needs a specifically sized area for the skids or landing gear to land safely. This is the footprint. The tail of the helicopter can extend beyond the footprint as it does not touch the ground.

MAST pants – medical antishock trousers used to constrict peripheral blood flow so that blood remains in a patient's torso where needed. Also used to stabilize leg and pelvic injuries. For years, the MAST, first named Military Anti-Shock Trousers, then later Medical Anti-Shock Trousers, were thought to work by actually transfusing blood from the legs back to the torso, then keeping it there. Studies showed that the transfusion was minimal. Also known as PASG, pneumatic anti-shock garment.

medevac – medical evacuation, it involves rescuing an injured person from areas difficult to access and can involve a litter team, helicopter shorthaul or other means of evacuation.

medic – a general reference to any ALS medical provider.

MI – myocardial infarction; death of heart muscle, commonly known as a heart attack.

military time – a standard for telling time that uses a 24-hour clock with hours referred to as hundreds; for example, noon is 1200 (twelve-hundred hours) and 1:00 p.m. is 1300 (thirteen-hundred hours).

Miller splint board – a shorter than average backboard that can float.

Miranda rights – legal rights of a person in custody to remain silent and to have an attorney present during questioning.

moraines – gravel and rocky debris left at the sides and ends of glaciers.

myocardial infarction – see *MI*.

needle thoracostomy – placing a catheter into the thoracic cavity in the second intercostal space, midline with the clavicle. Upon removal of the needle, air from a tension pneumothorax escapes, relieving pressure on the heart and lungs.

nitro – see *nitroglycerine.*

nitroglycerine – a medication given to patients with chest pain in an effort to increase perfusion to heart muscle.

nomex – a special fire resistant material worn by wildland firefighters and those who fly in park helicopters.

NPS – National Park Service.

operations – in the ICS, the person in charge of the details of the actual incident or emergency being dealt with, such as fireground operations or technical rescue.

orientation questions – asked of a patient to determine if they know who they are, where they are, the time and events of the situation.

oxygen saturation – see *sats.*

paramedic Emergency Medical Technician Paramedic provides advanced life support including advance airways, such as endotracheal intubation and surgical crichothryotomies; starts IVs and administers the range of medications in prehospital care; and provides advanced cardiac life support through EKG (electrocardiogram) interpretation and monitoring, and defibrillation.

Parkmedic – see *Intermediate EMT.*

PASG – pneumatic anti-shock garment; see *MAST pants.*

PBI – polybenzimidazole; see *PPE.*

pericardial tamponade – a condition caused by trauma where blood enters the sac around the heart and may eventually prevent the heart from contracting, resulting in death.

pericardiocentesis – the removal by syringe of blood from the sac around the heart so it may beat again.

personal protective equipment – see *PPE*.

pneumatic antishock garment – PASG; see *MAST pants*.

PPE – in structural firefighting, the turnouts made of nomex or PBI (polybenzimidazole), plus gloves, hood, helmet, SCBA, mask and boots.

prusik – a loop of small diameter rope that is secured to a larger diameter rope and brakes when tension is applied.

psi – pounds per square inch.

pulaski – a specialized wildland fire tool that is a combination axe and hoe.

SAR – search and rescue.

sats – oxygen saturation; a measurement of the amount of oxygen a patient's blood is carrying.

SCBA – self-contained breathing apparatus; the tank that structural firefighters wear to provide them with air when entering hazardous chemicals or smoky conditions.

sharps container – a container for used needles, wires, scalpels and other contaminated, sharp objects.

shock position – placing a patient on their back with their legs slightly elevated to keep blood in the torso.

shorthaul – to hang from below the helicopter for insertion into a rescue site.

Storz connector – a quick-connect adapter for connecting fire hose to hydrants.

streptokinase – a clot-buster medication used in the treatment of myocardial infarctions; this is used less often as cardiac catheterization becomes more available.

systolic blood pressure – the upper number in a blood pressure reading that indicates the pressure that blood is pumping through the system.

tension pneumothorax – a condition caused by trauma to the chest cavity. Air entering a lung exits through a tear in the lung and fills the closed thoracic or chest cavity. Eventually, the trapped chest air can squeeze the lung and heart to the side, resulting in death.

thrombolytics – medications used to dissolve clots (thrombosis) in blood vessels.

tone – a dispatch alert for a significant incident.

tone-outs – pager activation for a general alarm.

transport belt – a leather belt that is secured by a buckle around the waist of a person in custody. Their wrists are placed in hand-cuffs on the front of the belt. This is safer and more comfortable for a prisoner being transported for a long period of time.

turnouts – structural firefighter pants and jacket that are made of fire resistant material; also called bunkers.

water knot – a simple knot used to tie two ends of webbing together.